VIKING
TRANSFORMATION
KIT

BECOME A MODERN-DAY VIKING IN JUST 1 WEEK!

Viking Transformation Kit: Become a Modern-Day Viking in Just One Week!
1st Edition

Story concept, text, and compilation by © 2025 Kevin B. DiBacco

Editing, print preparation, formatting, back cover summary, cover and interior design provided by Page Turner Books, Inc.

Books may be ordered through popular, online retailers, the publisher's online store, IngramSpark, or by contacting the publisher at:

Page Turner Books, LLC
222 N. Lafayette St., Suite 11
Shelby, NC 28150

Visit our website at www.ptbooksinc.com or contact us via email at contact@ptbooksinc.com.

Page Turner Books, Inc. name and imprint are the trademark and copyright of Page Turner Books, Inc.

978-1-967289-52-3 (iBook & ePUB)
978-1-967289-53-0 (Hardcover)
978-1-967289-54-7 (Paperback)

Printed in the United States of America.

First printing: November 2025

VIKING
TRANSFORMATION
KIT

BECOME A MODERN-DAY
VIKING IN JUST 1 WEEK!

KEVIN B. DIBACCO

SHELBY, NC, USA

TABLE OF CONTENTS

FROM AVERAGE TO NORSE WARRIOR!

Greetings, potential Viking! If you're reading this, you've taken the first step on an epic journey that will transform you from a mild-mannered modern person into a fearsome Norse warrior.

DISCLAIMER

Results may vary. Side effects may include an inexplicable urge to grow a beard, even if you're not physically capable of doing so.

But why, you might ask, would anyone want to become a Viking in the 21st century? Well, let me counter with another question: Why *wouldn't* you?

Are you tired of dealing with rush hour traffic without the option of rowing away in a longship? Fed up with office politics that don't involve at least one axe? Frustrated by a lack of opportunities to shout "Skål!" in your day-to-day life? Then congratulations, my friend. This book is for you.

Now, I know what you're thinking. "But I don't know the first thing about being a Viking! I've never even pillaged a single village!" Fear not, oh uninitiated one. That's where this book comes in. We're going to take you on a journey from "Who's

1

Odin?" to "Odin's got nothing on me!" faster than you can say *Eyjafjallajökull*. That seemingly random assemblage of letters I just typed, is actually a real place in Iceland.

Before we dive into the nitty-gritty of Viking life, let's talk about what you can expect from this transformation.

SPOILER ALERT!
It's not going to be easy. You can't just throw on a horned helmet and call yourself a Norse warrior.

FUN FACT
Vikings didn't actually wear horned helmets.
Hollywood lied to you.

Oh, no. This will be a complete lifestyle overhaul. We're talking physical, mental, and spiritual changes. You're going to eat like a Viking, think like a Viking, and yes, smell like a Viking. Don't worry, we'll cover Viking hygiene practices. They were cleaner than you might think!

So, buckle up your fur-lined seatbelts because we're about to take you on a wild ride through every aspect of Viking life, adapted for the modern world.

HERE'S A SNEAK PEEK AT WHAT YOU'LL LEARN:

1. **Viking physique:** From Dad Bod to Rad Bod, we'll teach you how to transform your body from "couch potato" to "fierce warrior" without the need for actual battle. Expect workout routines that involve lifting heavy objects, rowing imaginary longships, and perfecting your war cry. By the end of this section, you'll be able to strike fear into the hearts of your enemies; or at least intimidate that guy who always takes your parking spot.

2. **Feast like a Norse god:** Forget your sad desk salads and microwave meals. We're going to introduce you to the Viking diet, full of hearty meats, robust stews, and enough mead to make even Odin say, "Whoa, take it easy there,

buddy." Don't worry, we'll also cover modern alternatives for those of you who prefer not to hunt your boar.

3. **Viking fashion—dressing to oppress:** Learn how to incorporate Norse style into your everyday wardrobe without looking like you got lost on your way to the Renaissance faire. We'll cover everything from subtle Viking accessories to full-on warrior gear.

   Warning! May result in confused looks from coworkers and spontaneous job offers from Medieval Times.

4. **The art of Viking conversation:** Master the art of speaking like a true Norse warrior. Learn essential phrases like "Prepare for battle!" and "Another mead, innkeeper!" We'll also teach you how to turn everyday conversation into epic sagas. Your friends will never ask how your weekend was without a touch of fear again.

5. **Viking home décor—Valhalla on a budget:** Transform your living space from "IKEA Showroom" to "Norse Great Hall" without breaking the bank. Learn how to incorporate shields into your wall decor, turn your coffee table into a miniature longship, and convince your roommates that a stuffed raven is a perfectly normal household pet.

6. **Modern Viking social life:** Navigate the treacherous waters of modern social interactions with the cunning of a Norse explorer. We'll cover everything from Viking-inspired pickup lines to how to turn your book club into a raiding party (metaphorically, of course – we don't condone actual pillaging).

7. **Career advice for the modern Viking:** Learn how to apply your newfound Viking skills to climb the corporate ladder. Master the art of the boardroom raid, perfect your power pose (**Hint:** It involves an imaginary axe), and learn how to

turn your performance reviews into epic sagas of your workplace heroics.

Now, I know what you're thinking. "This all sounds great, but can I really transform into a Viking? I mean, I get winded going up a flight of stairs, and the closest I've come to sailing the high seas is that time I got seasick aboard the ferry to Staten Island."

Well, my doubt-ridden friend, let me tell you a story…a saga if you will.

Once upon a time (last Tuesday, to be exact), there was an ordinary person named Alex. Alex worked in middle management, lived in a suburban apartment, and the most exciting thing in their life was the occasional extra shot of espresso in their morning latte.

But Alex had a dream.

A dream of something more.

A dream of…Vikings.

Alex bought this very book you're holding now.

At first, it seemed impossible. The workouts were tough, for who knew swinging a foam axe could be so tiring? The mead was an acquired taste as it turns out. You can't just chug it like soda. Alex's neighbors were less than thrilled about the attempts at backyard longship building.

But he persevered.

Day by day, workout by workout, feast by feast, Alex began to change. The dad bod transformed into a warrior physique. The meek office voice became a booming battle cry. The sparse apartment became a mini-Valhalla.

And then, one day, it happened.

Alex walked into work, beard braided, wearing subtle Viking-inspired accessories. Instead of meekly accepting extra work, Alex stood tall and declared, "I shall take on this mighty task, for Odin smiles upon the industrious!" The boss was so impressed by this newfound confidence that Alex got a promotion on the spot.

That weekend, instead of binge-watching Netflix, Alex went hiking with some new Viking enthusiast friends, seeing the natural world with new, Norse-inspired eyes. At the local pub's trivia night, Alex's team—The Valkyries—crushed the competition with their newfound knowledge of Norse history and mythology.

The moral of this saga? If Alex can do it, so can you. But be warned. The path to Viking-hood is not for the faint of heart. You will face many challenges along the way. You might strain a muscle trying to row an imaginary longship in your living room. You could accidentally call your boss "Jarl" in a meeting. You might clear out a party with your enthusiastic rendition of a Norse drinking song.

Fear not! For every challenge, this book offers a solution. Pulled a muscle? We've got Viking-inspired recovery techniques. Weirded out your boss? We've got tips for explaining your new lifestyle to confused colleagues. Offended the local bard with your singing? We've got guidelines for when and where it's proper to bust out your Norse vocals.

Now, let's address the longship in the room. You might be wondering, "Is this cultural appropriation? Am I going to offend people by doing this?" It's a valid concern, my culturally sensitive friend. But here's the thing, we're not here to mock or trivialize Viking culture. We're here to appreciate it, learn from it, and adapt its best aspects to modern life.

This book isn't about playing dress-up or using "I'm a Viking" as an excuse to act like a barbarian. It's about embracing the values that made the Vikings such a formidable and fascinating people. Things like:

1. Courage in the face of adversity, like when the office coffee machine breaks down.

2. A spirit of exploration and adventure, even if that just means trying a new route to work.

3. Strong community bonds. Your new Viking friends will be the best you've ever had.

4. Respect for nature. Vikings were surprisingly eco-friendly for their time.

5. Craftsmanship and pride in your work whether you're forging a sword or filing a report.

Throughout this book, we'll be drawing parallels between Viking life and modern life, showing you how to incorporate Norse wisdom into your daily routine without, you know, the less savory aspects of Viking history. We're aiming for "brave Norse warrior," not "violent pillager." Think less "conquer and plunder," more "explore and appreciate."

But let's be real for a moment. This journey isn't going to be all mead and longships. You're going to face some unique challenges as a modern Viking.

1. Explaining your new lifestyle to friends and family.

   "No, mom, I haven't joined a cult."

   "Yes, I know my beard is getting long."

2. Finding Viking-friendly workout spaces. Not every gym appreciates axe-throwing as cardio.

3. Adapting your diet. Turns out, it's harder than you'd think to find a whole roast boar these days.

4. Incorporating Norse style into a professional wardrobe.

   Hint: Maybe save the full fur cloak for casual Fridays.

5. Resisting the urge to solve all conflicts with a duel. HR generally frowns upon this, even if you use foam weapons.

But don't worry! This book will guide you through all these challenges and more. We'll teach you how to balance your Viking lifestyle with the demands of modern life. You'll learn to be a Viking in spirit, even when you can't be one in full battle gear.

And the best part? The skills you'll learn on this Viking journey are surprisingly applicable to modern life. That Viking confidence will serve you well in job interviews. The Norse appreciation for nature might inspire you to finally take that camping trip you've been putting off. The Viking spirit of community could lead you to form the tightest-knit group of friends you've ever had. And let's be honest, being able to casually drop Norse mythology references into conversation is a fantastic way to seem mysterious and interesting at parties.

Now, I know some of you might be thinking, "This all sounds great, but I'm not sure I have what it takes to be a Viking. I mean, I can barely grow a beard, I'm afraid of boats, and the sight of blood makes me queasy."

First of all, not all Vikings had beards. There were plenty of fierce Viking women warriors, and I'm quite sure most of them didn't have facial hair. Secondly, you don't need to be on a boat to have the heart of a Viking explorer. Your territory for exploration might be your city, or the great wilderness of your local park. And as for the blood... well, we're not actually going to be doing any real raiding or pillaging, so you can rest easy on that front.

The point is anyone can embrace the Viking spirit. It's not about looking a certain way or having specific skills. It's about attitude. It's about facing life's challenges with the courage of someone who would sail into unknown waters on a wooden ship. It's about approaching your daily life with the curiosity and wonder of an explorer discovering new lands. It's about treating your friends and family with the loyalty and respect that Viking clans showed to their own.

So, are you ready to begin your transformation? Are you prepared to journey from mild-mannered modern person to fierce Norse warrior? Are you willing to put in the work, face the challenges, and possibly explain to your neighbors why you're trying to park a longship in your driveway?

If you answered yes or *"Skål!"* which we'll accept as an enthusiastic affirmative, then turn the page and let your Viking journey begin. But before you do, a few final words of advice.

1. Remember, it's about the journey, not the destination. You're not going to wake up one day and suddenly be a Viking. It's a process, and every step is an adventure in itself.

2. Don't take yourself too seriously. Yes, we want you to embrace the Viking spirit, but if you find yourself genuinely angry that the local coffee shop doesn't accept payment in hack-silver, you might be taking things a bit too far.

3. Be prepared for some strange looks, confused questions, and possibly an intervention staged by concerned friends. Also, be prepared for new friendships, exciting experiences, and a life lived with more passion and purpose than you ever thought possible.

4. Finally, and most importantly, always remember the Viking motto: "Row first, ask questions later." Okay, that wasn't really their motto, but it sounds cool, doesn't it?

So, grab your imaginary axe, straighten your non-existent horned helmet, and get ready to Viking-ify your life! *Skål*, and happy raiding! (Metaphorically speaking, of course. *We cannot stress enough how much we don't condone actual raiding.)*

CHAPTER 1

So, You Want to Be a Viking, Eh?

Greetings, brave soul! Welcome to *Viking Transformation Kit—Become a Modern-Day Viking in Less Than a Week!* If you've picked up this book, you're either a history buff with a deep sense of humor, someone who's watched one too many episodes of *Vikings*, or just a regular person who's decided that the modern world is overrated, and it's time to embrace your inner Norseman. Whatever your reason, congratulations! You're about to embark on a hilarious journey through time, space, and IKEA as we explore the art of bringing the Viking lifestyle into the 21st century.

Now, before we dive into the fjords of fun, let's get one thing straight. *No actual pillaging is required or necessary.*

First things first, we need to address the longship in the room. Despite what you may have heard, being a modern Viking does NOT involve:

1. Actual pillaging. Sorry if this disappoints you.

2. Raiding coastal monasteries: They have terrible Wi-Fi anyway.

3. Kidnapping monks. They're not the best conversationalists.

4. Burning villages. Marshmallow roasts are allowed, though.

5. Time travel. We're working on it, but the technology just isn't there yet.

What we're aiming for here is more of a Viking-inspired lifestyle, minus the less savory aspects of historical Norse culture. Think of it as "Viking Light" or "I Can't Believe It's Not Plunder." We're taking the best parts of Viking culture—the epic beards, the cool clothes, the badass attitude—and leaving behind the parts that would get you arrested in modern society.

So, if you're looking for a guide on how to steal your neighbor's cow or navigate a longship through international waters without a permit, I'm afraid you've come to the wrong place. However, if you're interested in learning how to rock a beard that would make Odin jealous, throw a feast that would impress Thor himself, or simply inject a little more adventure into your daily life, then strap on your hornless helmet and prepare for a wild ride!

Remember, the goal here is to have fun, learn a bit about history, and impress your friends at the next costume party. No actual harming of monks or pillaging of villages is endorsed by the author, the publisher, or any respectable mead hall.

Why go Viking in the modern world?

You might be wondering, "In a world of smartphones, electric cars, and avocado toast, why on earth would I want to embrace the lifestyle of people who lived over a thousand years ago?"

Well, my soon-to-be-bearded friend, allow me to enlighten you on the many benefits of bringing a little Viking flair into your 21st-century life.

1. Instant respect (or fear) from your neighbors: Imagine that you're at your neighborhood barbecue, and instead of showing up in cargo shorts and a "Kiss the Cook" apron, you arrive in full Viking regalia, complete with a massive beard and a battleaxe (plastic, of course—remember our disclaimer). Suddenly, you're not just "Bob from two doors down." You're "Bob the Fearsome," and people are lining up to make sure you get first dibs on the potato salad.

2. A foolproof excuse for your man cave: "Honey, it's not a man cave, it's a mead hall." Boom. Argument won.

3. The ultimate ice breaker: Tired of awkward small talk at parties? Try introducing yourself as a modern Viking. You'll either have a fascinating conversation or clear the room entirely. Either way, problem solved!

4. A new perspective on home décor: Why settle for mass-produced wall art when you can adorn your living room with shields and crossed swords? It's not clutter; it's cultural appreciation.

5. The best Halloween costume ever: Once you've fully embraced the Viking lifestyle, you'll never have to worry about what to wear for Halloween again. Plus, you can subtly judge all those who show up in historically inaccurate Viking costumes.

6. An excuse to grow epic facial hair: Have you always wanted to grow a beard that could house a family of sparrows, but never had a good reason? Well, now you do. It's not laziness; it's commitment to your new lifestyle.

7. A whole new workout routine, forget CrossFit: Viking-inspired workouts are the new trend. Swinging battleaxes (foam, for safety) and lifting mead barrels will give you a warrior's physique in no time.

8. An appreciation for the simple things: In a world of constant digital stimulation, embracing Viking culture can help you appreciate the simpler things in life, like a well-crafted wooden bowl or the satisfaction of starting a fire without burning down your entire neighborhood.

9. A built-in community: Join the growing community of modern Viking enthusiasts. Bond over beard-grooming tips, mead recipes, and historically inaccurate TV shows. It's like a book club, but with more drinking horns.

10. A legitimate reason to buy a boat: Always wanted a boat but couldn't justify the expense? Well, every Viking needs a vessel. Just don't call it a yacht—it's a longship.

11. Improved problem-solving skills: When faced with a problem, you can always ask yourself, "What would a Viking do?" (Just be sure to filter the answer through modern laws and social norms.)

12. A new appreciation for winter: Vikings didn't let a little thing like freezing temperatures stop them. Embrace the cold and you'll never complain about winter again. You might still complain, but you'll do it in a much more poetic, Norse-inspired way.

13. An excuse for epic feasts: Viking culture is all about communal eating and drinking. It's the perfect excuse to gather your friends for regular feasts. Just remember it's not overeating, it's cultural immersion.

14. A renewed sense of adventure: Vikings were explorers at heart. Embracing Viking culture might just give you the push you need to step out of your comfort zone and explore the world (or at least the next county over).

15. The joy of anachronism: There's something inherently funny about applying ancient Norse solutions to modern problems. Stuck in traffic? A Viking would abandon their car and row to work!

So, you see, going Viking in the modern world isn't about wearing funny hats or drinking out of horns (although those are perks). It's about embracing a sense of adventure, community, and self-reliance that's often lacking in our digital age. It's about injecting a bit of warrior spirit into your daily life, even if the only things you're battling are rush hour traffic and passive-aggressive emails.

Plus, let's be honest, it's plain fun. In a world that often takes itself too seriously, deciding to become a modern Viking is a fantastic way to rebel against the mundane. So, grab your imaginary sword, polish your non-existent helmet, and get ready to Viking-ify your life!

A BRIEF, HILARIOUS HISTORY OF VIKINGS

Before we dive into the intricacies of modern Viking life, let's take a quick, slightly irreverent look at the history of these Norse warriors. Buckle up because this isn't your high school history teacher's Viking lesson (unless your history teacher was really, cool).

THE VIKING AGE: Not Just a Phase, Mom! The Viking Age officially kicked off in 793 AD when a bunch of Norse fellows decided that the quiet monastery of Lindisfarne, off the coast of England, could use some unexpected visitors. This wasn't so much a planned historical epoch as it was a group of guys saying, "Hey, you know what would be fun? Sailing across the sea and taking other people's stuff!" And thus, a legend was born.

LONGSHIPS: The SUVs of the Middle Ages, Vikings were known for their impressive ships, which were like the Swiss

Army knives of sea vessels. Need to navigate shallow rivers? Check. Want to carry a ton of loot? No problem. Fancy a bit of speed for quick getaways? You got it. These ships were so versatile that if Vikings had bumper stickers, they'd read "My other car is a longship."

VIKING FASHION: Ahead of their time, contrary to widespread belief, Vikings didn't wear horned helmets. This was a 19th-century invention, probably by someone who thought, "You know what would make these fearsome warriors even more intimidating? Impractical headgear!" In reality, Viking fashion was quite practical and, dare we say, stylish? They were rocking the layered look long before it was cool, and their bling game was strong with intricate brooches and arm rings.

NORSE MYTHOLOGY: Game of Thrones, eat your heart out! Norse myths are full of drama, betrayal, and family feuds that make modern soap operas look tame. You've got Odin, the one-eyed Allfather who's always up for trading body parts for wisdom. There's Thor, whose solution to every problem is to hit it with a hammer (a strategy still employed by some today). And let's not forget Loki, the original trickster who makes modern-day pranksters look like amateurs.

VIKING NAME FUN FACT: "Viking" wasn't actually what these Norse people called themselves. It was more of a job description, like "teacher" or "plumber," but for people who went on raids. So, saying "I'm going Viking" was like saying "I'm going plumbing," but with more axes and less... well, plumbing.

EXPLORATION: Mistakes Were Made, Greenland Was Named, Vikings were excellent explorers, reaching as far as North America long before Columbus. However, their naming skills left something to be desired. CASE IN POINT: Greenland. Erik the Red, in what might be history's first case of misleading real estate advertising, named this ice-covered land "Greenland" to attract settlers. One can only imagine the disappointment of those early colonists.

"Wait, this isn't the lush paradise we were promised! Erik, you've got some explaining to do!"

THE END OF AN ERA

ALL GOOD THINGS MUST COME TO AN END

The Viking Age wound down around the 11th century. Reasons for this include the spread of Christianity, the strengthening of European kingdoms, and possibly the realization that there were easier ways to make a living than sailing across stormy seas to take other people's stuff. Plus, all that pillaging must have been exhausting.

LEGACY

MORE THAN JUST HORNED HELMETS AND LONGSHIPS

Despite their relatively brief time in the spotlight, the Vikings left a lasting impact on the world. They founded cities, influenced languages, and left behind a rich cultural heritage. They also gave us some great vocabulary words like "berserk," "ransack," and "slaughter" – you know, for those days when you really need to express yourself.

So, there you have it – a brief and highly amusing (if not 100% historically correct) look at Viking history. Remember, like any good Viking, we've plundered the facts and reshaped them for our purposes. But don't worry, no monks were harmed in the writing of this section.

WHAT TO EXPECT FROM THIS GUIDE

Now that we've covered why you should embrace your inner Viking and taken a whirlwind tour through Viking history, you might be wondering, "What exactly am I getting myself into with this book?" Well, fearless reader, allow me to give you a sneak peek into the adventure that awaits you in the pages ahead.

1. **A complete Viking makeover:** We'll start by transforming you from a regular 21st-century person into a fearsome (yet oddly charming) modern Viking. Expect tips on growing the perfect beard, braiding techniques that would make a Valkyrie jealous, and how to rock Viking-inspired fashion without looking like you're permanently en route to a costume party.

2. **Fitness tips for the modern raider:** Discover workout routines that will give you the strength to metaphorically pillage your way through life's challenges. We'll cover everything from "Longship Rowing" (a killer cardio workout) to "Boulder Toss" (who needs dumbbells when you have... well, boulders?).

3. **Feasting like a Norse god:** Learn to throw dinner parties that would impress Odin himself. We'll explore Nordic-inspired cuisine that goes beyond just meat on a stick, and yes, we'll teach you how to make mead without accidentally creating a biohazard in your bathtub.

4. **Viking etiquette for the modern world:** Discover how to channel your inner Viking without getting arrested. We'll cover important topics like "When is it appropriate to challenge someone to a duel?" (SPOILER: Almost never) and "How to attend a business meeting with an axe" (SPOILER: Don't).

5. **Home décor—Valhalla on a budget:** Transform your living space into a Norse paradise. Learn how to incorporate shields into your wall decor without compromising your security deposit and discover the joy of drinking from horns without spilling mead all over your carpet.

6. **Viking problem-solving:** Approach modern problems with the Viking spirit. Stuck in traffic? We'll teach you how to let out a war cry without alarming fellow commuters. Dealing with difficult coworkers? Learn the art of writing passive-aggressive runes.

7. **Building your clan:** Tips on finding like-minded Viking enthusiasts in your area, and how to form a modern-day "raiding party" (aka a very intense book club).

8. **Viking mindfulness—because even a warrior needs to chill sometimes.** Learn meditation techniques that don't conflict with your new badass image.

THROUGHOUT THIS GUIDE, YOU'LL FIND:

- Hilarious anecdotes from fellow modern Vikings.

- 'What Would a Viking Do?' scenarios to test your newfound Norse knowledge.

- Translations of modern phrases into Old Norse (perfect for confusing your friends).

- Tips on explaining your new lifestyle to bewildered family members.

Remember, this guide is meant to be as entertaining as it is informative. We're not aiming for historical accuracy here (sorry, history buffs), but rather a fun, light-hearted approach to injecting some Viking spirit into modern life.

So, sharpen your wit (since we can't actually sharpen axes), grab your reading horn (it's like reading glasses, but more Viking-y), and prepare to embark on a journey that's part self-help, part history, and all ridiculous fun. Skál!

THE VIKING CODE

NINE NOBLE VIRTUES FOR THE MODERN AGE

Before we set sail on our grand adventure into modern Viking life, it's worth taking a moment to understand the core values that guided our Norse ancestors. The Vikings, contrary to widely held belief, weren't just about pillaging and plundering. They had a strong moral code known as the NINE NOBLE VIRTUES. Let's take a look at these virtues and how we can hilariously apply them to our 21st-century lives.

1. **Courage:** In Viking times, this meant facing sea monsters and enemy warriors. For us, modern Vikings, it's about facing your boss when asking for a raise or trying that questionable sushi from the gas station.

2. **Truth:** Vikings valued honesty. In the modern world, this translates to admitting when you've binge-watched an entire series instead of doing your chores. Your longhouse (apartment) might be a mess, but at least you're truthful!

3. **Honor:** For Vikings, this meant upholding their reputation. For us, it's about honoring our commitments, like actually going to the gym after paying for that membership. Your ancestors didn't row across oceans for you to skip leg day!

4. **Fidelity:** Vikings were loyal to their clan. In modern terms, this could mean staying faithful to your favorite sports team, even when they're having a season so bad it makes you want to pillage something.

5. **Discipline:** Viking discipline was about mastering skills and self-control. For us, it's resisting the urge to check social media every five minutes or not hitting the snooze button for the fifth time. Remember, Odin is watching!

6. **Hospitality:** Vikings believed in being generous hosts. In the 21st century, this doesn't mean sharing your plunder, but it could mean actually cleaning your apartment before guests arrive instead of just shoving everything into the closet.

7. **Industriousness:** Vikings worked hard at their crafts. For modern Vikings, this means giving your all at work, even if your job is less "forging mighty weapons" and more "forging mighty spreadsheets."

8. **Self-reliance:** Vikings valued independence. In today's world, this could translate to learning to cook instead of surviving on takeout or finally figuring out how to do your own taxes without calling your parents.

9. **Perseverance:** Vikings never gave up, whether battling storms at sea or enemy hordes. For us, it's about not giving up when learning a new skill, like mastering the art of the perfect man bun or finally figuring out how to assemble that IKEA furniture without leftover parts.

By embracing these NINE NOBLE VIRTUES in our modern context, we're not just playing dress-up – we're channeling the true spirit of the Vikings. It's about facing life's challenges with the heart of a warrior, even if the scariest thing you'll face today is your inbox on a Monday morning.

THE MODERN VIKING TOOLKIT

ESSENTIAL ITEMS FOR YOUR JOURNEY

Now that you're committed to embracing your inner Viking, you might be wondering what gear you'll need for this quest. Fear not, brave soul! Here's a list of essential items every modern Viking should have in their arsenal.

1. **A mighty beard comb:** Your beard is your pride and joy. Treat it with the respect it deserves. A good beard comb is like a sword for your face — it helps you conquer the wild tangle of facial hair and emerge victorious.

2. **Smartphone with Norse Runes keyboard:** Because a Norse "modern Viking" sends text messages in ancient Norse. "Hey, you up?" becomes a mystical incantation when written in runes.

3. **A drinking horn (travel size):** Perfect for sipping your morning coffee or evening mead.

   Warning: May cause confused looks from baristas.

4. **Viking-inspired workout gear:** Swap your regular gym clothes for fur-lined workout gear. Nothing motivates you to lift heavy quite like channeling your inner berserker.

5. **A pocket guide to Norse mythology:** For those times when you need to casually drop Odin's wisdom into conversation or decide which Norse god to blame for your misfortunes.

6. **A collapsible battle axe (foam edition):** For impromptu epic pose or settling disputes over the last slice of pizza.

   REMEMBER: Foam only — we're modern Vikings, not barbarians.

7. **Noise-canceling headphones:** Because even a Viking needs peace every so often. Plus, they look a bit like helmet earmuffs, which is totally on-brand.

8. **A stylish man-bag (or shield if you prefer):** For carrying all your modern Viking essentials. Bonus points if it's shaped like a shield.

9. **Business cards with a Norse-inspired title:** "John Smith, Software Developer" becomes "Jón Smithson, Digital Rune Carver." Networking has never been this entertaining.

10. **A flashlight (because torches are a fire hazard):** All the illumination with none of the risk of setting your apartment on fire. Odin would approve of this safety-conscious choice.

Remember, being a modern Viking is all about balance. You're walking the line between two worlds – the ancient and the modern. It's about bringing the best of Norse culture into your everyday life while still being a functioning member of 21st-century society.

POTENTIAL PITFALLS ON YOUR VIKING JOURNEY

As with any great saga, your journey to becoming a modern Viking will have its challenges. Here are some potential pitfalls.

1. **The overzealous battle cry:** While letting out a mighty "Skål!" before taking a sip of your drink is acceptable, doing so in a quiet café might earn you some strange looks. Remember, timing is everything.

2. **The beard mishap:** Growing a Viking beard is an art. There's a fine line between "majestic Norse god" and "castaway who's lost his razor." Regular grooming is key.

3. **The mead over-enthusiast:** Mead is delicious, but remember – you're aiming for "merry Viking," not "Viking who can't find his longship." Drink responsibly.

4. **The oversharing of Norse knowledge:** While your newfound expertise on Norse mythology is impressive, not everyone wants to hear about Thor's goat-drawn chariot during casual small talk.

5. **The axe accident:** Foam axes are fun but swinging them in confined spaces can lead to broken lamps and strained friendships. Always be aware of your surroundings.

6. **The language barrier:** Peppering your speech with Old Norse words is cool but make sure you're using them correctly. You don't want to accidentally challenge your boss to a holmgang (duel) when you meant to ask for a raise.

7. **The fashion faux pas:** Viking-inspired fashion can be great, but there's a time and place. A full fur cloak might not be appropriate for your cousin's wedding in July.

8. **The overcommitment to the lifestyle:** Remember, you're a modern Viking. It's okay to use modern conveniences. You don't need to row to work or hunt your own food (unless you want to, of course).

By being aware of these potential pitfalls, you'll be better equipped to navigate the tricky waters of modern Viking life. Remember, it's all about finding the right balance between your Norse inspiration and your contemporary reality.

EMBARKING ON YOUR VIKING ADVENTURE

And there you have it, brave modern Viking! You're now armed with the knowledge to begin your journey into the world of contemporary Norse living. Remember, this guide is meant to be as entertaining as it is 'informative.' We're not here to recreate history with 100% accuracy (sorry, historians), but to inject a bit of Viking spirit into our everyday lives.

As you read through the coming chapters, keep in mind that being a modern Viking is about more than just growing a beard or drinking from a horn (though those are certainly fun parts of it). It's about embracing the Viking spirit of adventure, community, and resilience. It's about facing life's challenges with the heart of a warrior, even if the scariest thing you'll face today is a tough work presentation or a first date.

So, whether you're reading this book to spice up your life, to find a new hobby, or just for a good laugh, remember to approach it with the Viking spirit of fun and adventure. Don't be afraid to laugh at yourself as you try out these Viking-inspired lifestyle tips. After all, if Vikings could face sea monsters and rival clans, you can certainly face the embarrassment of accidentally saying "Skål!" in a business meeting.

In the words of a great Viking philosopher (okay, I made that up), "Life is too short not to live it like a Viking." So, grab your metaphorical axe, straighten your imaginary horned helmet, and get ready to conquer the modern world, one hilarious Viking-inspired adventure at a time.

Skål, and happy raiding (metaphorically, of course)!

CHAPTER 2

VIKING PHYSIQUE: FROM DAD BOD TO RAID BOD

Imagine you're standing in front of your bathroom mirror, your newly grown beard glistening with artisanal beard oil. You've got the Viking look down pat – the wild hair, the rugged clothes, maybe even a toy axe propped up against the sink (don't worry, we won't tell anyone it's made of foam). But as you turn to the side and suck in your gut, you realize there's one minor problem with your Viking transformation.

Actually, it might not be such a slight problem after all.

That's right, my friend. I'm talking about your physique. While your enthusiasm for Norse culture is as vast as the Nordic seas, your belly is… well, let's just say it's giving off more "Santa Claus" vibes than "Thor, God of Thunder." But fear not, aspiring Viking! This chapter is all about transforming your body from "Dad Bod" to "Raid Bod."

Now, before we dive into the nitty-gritty of Viking fitness, let's address the elephant (or should I say, the bilgesnipe) in the room. Despite what Hollywood might have you believe, not all

Vikings were chiseled Adonises with washboard abs and biceps the size of tree trunks. In reality, Viking physiques were probably as varied as their raids were wide-ranging. Some were undoubtedly buff from all that rowing and axe-swinging, while others might have been a bit softer around the edges thanks to all that mead and feasting.

But here's the thing — we're not aiming for historical accuracy here. We're aiming for the Viking ideal, the kind of body that makes you feel like you could row across the Atlantic and throw a hammer into the stratosphere or hold up a shield wall against a horde of angry Saxons. And let's be honest, we're also aiming for the kind of body that looks damn good in a leather vest.

So, how do we get there? Well, my soon-to-be-buff buddy, we're going to take a page out of the Viking playbook and create a workout regimen that would make even the burliest berserker break a sweat. But don't worry — no actual pillaging or plundering required. We're going to raid the gym instead of villages, and the only thing we'll be conquering is our own limitations.

Let's start with the cornerstone of any Viking's fitness routine: rowing. Now, I know what you're thinking. "But I don't have a longship!" Well, unless you live in a very understanding neighborhood with a conveniently located fjord, we're going to have to make do with the next best thing: the rowing machine.

Ah, the rowing machine. That strange contraption gathering dust in the corner of your gym, ignored by all except the most dedicated fitness enthusiasts and confused newcomers who think it might be some sort of torture device. Well, my friend, it's time to make that machine your new best friend. Think of it as your very own portable longship, minus the dragon head and the risk of seasickness.

"LONGSHIP ROWING"

The **"Longship Rowing"** workout is simple in theory but brutal in practice.

Start with a 5-minute warm-up at a moderate pace. Then, imagine you're a Viking on a raid. You've just spotted a wealthy monastery on the horizon, and you need to get there before the monks can hide all their gold.

Now **row like your plunder depends on it! Go all out for 30 seconds, then recover at a slower pace for 90 seconds.**

Repeat this cycle 8 times, or until you feel like you've crossed the North Sea.

As you're huffing and puffing on the rowing machine, red-faced and wondering why on earth you thought this Viking thing was an innovative idea, just remember that every pull is bringing you closer to your Viking physique. And hey, at least you don't have to worry about splinters from wooden oars or surprise attacks from rival clans.

But a true Viking warrior isn't just about rowing strength. Oh no, we need to work on those arms too. After all, you never know when you might need to throw a hammer at a frost giant or arm wrestle Thor himself. That's where our next exercise comes in.

"HAMMER THROW FOR KILLER ARMS"

Now, before you get too excited, I should clarify that we're not actually going to be throwing hammers. Your local gym probably frowns upon that sort of thing, and we want to build muscle, not a criminal record. Instead, we're going to use a medicine ball to simulate the action of hammer throwing.

Find an open space (preferably outdoors, to minimize property damage and maximize your connection with nature), grab a **medicine ball**, and channel your inner Thor. The technique is simple.

Hold the ball with both hands, swing it back between your legs, then explosively swing it up and over your head, releasing it at the top of the arc. Just be sure to warn any nearby pedestrians. Nothing ruins a workout quite like concussing an innocent bystander.

Start with 3 sets of 10 throws, alternating sides. As you get stronger, increase the weight of the ball or the number of repetitions. Before you know it, you'll have arms that would make Chris Hemsworth jealous. Just remember to balance out your training – we don't want you ending up lopsided like a Viking who's been rowing on the same side of the longship for too long.

Now, I know what you're thinking. "But what about my core? How am I supposed to rock a Viking beard if I can't even rock a six-pack?" Well, my ab-seeking amigo, that's where our next exercise comes in.

SHIELD WALL PLANKS

In actual Viking battles, the shield wall was a defensive formation where warriors would overlap their shields to create an impenetrable barrier. In our workout, we're going to create a different kind of wall – a wall of steel-hard abdominal muscles that could deflect sword blows (not that we recommend testing this theory).

The **Shield Wall Plank** is a variation on the standard plank exercise.

Start in a standard plank position, forearms on the ground, body straight as a Viking's sword. But here's where it gets interesting – imagine you're holding up a heavy wooden shield with your back.

Every 30 seconds, shift your weight to one side, as if you're repositioning your shield to block an incoming attack. **Hold for 5 seconds, then return to center.**

Alternate sides until your abs feel like they're on fire (or until you collapse in a heap, whichever comes first).

As you're quivering in this position, face red, sweat dripping onto your yoga mat, just imagine how impressed your ancestors would be. Sure, they might be a bit confused about why you're lying on the floor of a climate-controlled room instead of fighting off invaders, but they'd definitely appreciate the effort.

Now, I know what some of you might be thinking. "This all sounds great, but I'm more of a lone wolf than a gym rat. How can I get a Viking body without leaving my homestead?" Well, fear not, my introverted innovator! The Vikings were nothing if not resourceful, and we can channel that same spirit into creating a home workout that would make even the most hardcore gym-goer raise an impressed eyebrow.

"RAID YOUR HOUSE"

Welcome to what I like to call the **"Raid Your House"** workout. It's time to look at your humble abode through the eyes of a Viking raider. That heavy coffee table? Perfect for deadlifts. Those stairs? Your new cardio machine. That bag of pet food? Congratulations, you've just discovered the Viking version of a kettlebell.

Start your home raid with the **"Couch Crusher"**.
Stand at one end of your couch, **squat** down, and **lift** one end off the ground. **Hold for 30 seconds**, then gently lower it.
Rest for 30 seconds, then repeat on the other end. Not only will this work your legs and back, but it's also a wonderful way to find all the loose change and lost TV remotes that have disappeared into the couch void.

Next, move on to the **"Bookshelf Row"**.
Stand facing your bookshelf, grab the edges, and lean back at a 45-degree angle.
Pull yourself in, as if you're trying to steal knowledge itself. Bonus points if you actually read a few lines from a book with each rep. Who says Vikings can't be intellectuals?

For cardio, we have the **"Stairway to Valhalla"**.
Simply **run up and down your stairs as many times as you can in 5 minutes**. If you live in a single-story home or apartment, fear not! You can substitute this with the "Floor is Lava" exercise. Pretend your floor is covered in, well, lava, and

leap from one piece of furniture to another. Just be sure to put away any breakables first. We're going for "Viking warrior," not "bull in a China shop."

Finally, end your home workout with the **"Laundry Basket Battle."**

Fill a laundry basket with clothes (clean or dirty, we don't judge) and carry it around your house as if you're hauling plunder back to your longship. For an extra challenge, try this while wearing socks on a smooth floor – it's like ice skating, but with more risk of embarrassing yourself in front of your pets.

Remember, the key to any good workout routine is consistency. **Try to raid your house at least three times a week.** Before you know it, you'll have the strength to rearrange your furniture on a whim and the endurance to carry all your groceries in one trip. Your roommates or family members might think you've gone slightly mad, but they'll appreciate your newfound ability to open stubborn jar lids.

Now, I know we've been focusing a lot on building strength and endurance, but there's one more aspect of the Viking physique we need to address: flexibility. That's right, my friend. Contrary to widespread belief, Vikings weren't just muscle-bound brutes. They needed to be agile to navigate longships, dodge enemy attacks, and, of course, to execute those complex Viking dance moves at post-raid parties (okay, I made that last one up, but can you imagine?).

So, let's round out our Viking fitness routine with some Norse-inspired stretches. We'll call this part of the workout **"Loki's Yoga"** – because like the trickster god himself, you'll be twisting yourself into shapes you never thought possible.

"LOKI'S YOGA"

Start with the **"Odin's Spear"** pose.

Stand straight, then bend forward, keeping your legs straight and reaching for your toes. As you're down there, wobbling like a newborn calf, just imagine you're Odin, reaching down to Earth to impart wisdom (or to pick up that TV remote you dropped during your "Couch Crusher" exercise).

Next, move into the **"Thor's Hammer"** stretch.
Interlace your fingers behind your back, then lift your arms as high as you can, puffing out your chest.
Hold this pose while imagining you're Thor, raising Mjölnir to summon lightning. The burning you feel in your shoulders. That's just the power of the gods coursing through you (or possibly a sign that you need to stretch more often).

Finally, end with the **"World Serpent"** twist.
Sit on the floor with your legs straight out in front of you.
Bend your right knee and place your right foot on the outside of your left thigh.
Then, twist your torso to the right, placing your left elbow on the outside of your right knee. As you hold this twist, imagine you're the World Serpent, Jörmungandr, wrapping yourself around the Earth. Just try not to actually hiss while you're doing it – your neighbors might start to worry.

And there you have it, my Viking-in-training! A complete workout routine to take you from "Dad Bod" to "Raid Bod." Remember, the path to a Viking physique is not an easy one. There will be sweat. There will be sore muscles. There may even be some questionable grunting noises that make your family members check on you to make sure you haven't actually been transported back to the Age of Vikings.

But with persistence, dedication, and a healthy dose of humor, you'll soon find yourself transformed. Your arms will be strong enough to row across oceans (or at least to win a few arm-wrestling matches at your local mead hall). Your core will be solid enough to withstand the fiercest of battles (or the most vigorous of belly laughs). And your legs will have the power to carry you through the longest of raids (or the most grueling of Black Friday sales).

So go forth, my burgeoning berserker, and conquer your fitness goals with the ferocity of a Viking raid. And remember, in the immortal words of a great Viking philosopher (who may or may not be entirely fictional): "The pain you feel today will be the strength you feel tomorrow. Also, mead tastes better when you've earned it."

Now, if you'll excuse me, all this writing about exercise has made me tired. I think it's time for a nice, relaxing Viking power nap. Right after I finish this horn of mead, of course. Skål!

Chapter 3

Feast Like a Norse God

Picture this: It's been a long day of metaphorical raiding (aka your 9-to-5 job), and you've just finished your "Raid Your House" workout. Your muscles are aching, your beard is glistening with sweat, and your stomach is growling louder than Thor's thunder. It's time to feast like a Norse god.

But wait! Before you reach for that sad microwave dinner or dial for yet another pizza, let's remember that you're a Viking now. And Vikings don't settle for mundane meals. Oh, no. Vikings turn every meal into an epic saga, a culinary adventure worthy of the skalds' songs. So put down that frozen burrito, my hungry hero, and let's embark on a gastronomic journey that would make Odin himself salivate.

Now, you might be thinking, "But I can't cook! The last time I tried to make something more complicated than toast, I nearly burned down my apartment!" Fear not, my culinary challenged comrade. By the end of this chapter, you'll be wielding kitchen utensils with the same confidence a Viking wields his battle axe. Speaking of which...

Let's start with the most valuable tool in any modern Viking's kitchen arsenal: the Pizza Battle Axe. That's right, you heard me. Gone are the days of flimsy pizza wheels that barely cut through the crust. As a Viking, you need something with a bit more... oomph.

Now, before you rush off to your local kitchenware store asking for a "Pizza Battle Axe," let me clarify. We're not talking about an actual axe here. (Remember, we're trying to prepare a meal, not re-enact a battle scene.) What we're looking for is a sturdy cleaver or a heavy-duty pizza cutter that you can dramatically raise above your head before bringing it down with a satisfying "thwack" on your pizza.

Imagine you and your friends are gathered in your living room, eagerly awaiting their share of the feast. You emerge from the kitchen, pizza in one hand, cleaver in the other. With a mighty cry of "Behold! I bring sustenance!" you raise the cleaver high, then bring it down in one swift motion, cleaving the pizza into perfect slices. Your friends gasp in awe. You've just elevated a simple pizza night into an epic Norse saga.

But a true Viking feast isn't just about the theatrics (although, let's be honest, the theatrics are pretty fun). It's about hearty, satisfying food that can fuel a warrior through long nights of... binge-watching Norse mythology documentaries on Netflix. So, let's talk about how to Viking-ify some of your favorite modern dishes.

THE MIGHTY MEATBALL MJOLNIR: Traditional Swedish meatballs get a Thor-inspired upgrade. Shape your meatballs into little hammers (or as close as you can get – no one's expecting sculptural perfection here), then serve them on a bed of mashed potatoes with a generous helping of gravy. As you're about to dig in, don't forget to solemnly intone, "I deem this meal worthy," while holding a meatball aloft. Bonus points if you can get your dining companions to respond with a hearty "Huzzah!"

THE LONGSHIP SUB: Take your favorite submarine sandwich and turn it into a seaworthy vessel. Use a long baguette as the base of your ship, then load it up with your preferred meats, cheeses, and vegetables. The trick is in the presentation: cut a narrow V-shape out of each end of the baguette to form the bow and stern of your ship. Use slices of bell pepper or carrot to create oars along the sides. For the final addition, stab a toothpick with a small piece of cheese into one end as your sail. Voilà! You've got a sandwich that's ready to sail the seven seas... or at least make it from your plate to your mouth.

ODIN'S ONE-EYED BREAKFAST SANDWICH: Take your standard breakfast sandwich – egg, cheese, and your choice of bacon or sausage – but here's the Viking twist: use a single fried egg with the yolk intact to represent Odin's one eye. As you assemble your sandwich, regale your half-awake family or roommates with the tale of how Odin sacrificed his eye for wisdom. Nothing says "good morning" quite like a mythological monologue over coffee.

Now, I know we've been focusing a lot on meat-heavy dishes, but let's not forget that Vikings were also farmers and foragers.

For our vegetarian Vikings (yes, they exist!), I present the **YGGDRASIL SALAD BOWL:** Create a layered salad in a clear bowl, with each layer representing a different realm of the world tree. Dark leafy greens at the bottom for the roots stretching into Niflheim, a layer of nuts and seeds for Midgard, and top it off with colorful fruits and edible flowers for the canopy reaching into Asgard. As you eat, you can contemplate the interconnectedness of all things... or just enjoy the fact that you're eating a salad out of something other than a sad plastic container at your desk.

But what's a feast without something to wash it all down? While mead might be the traditional Viking beverage of choice, not everyone has a horn of honeyed wine lying around. So, let's get creative with some modern alternatives.

THE FROST GIANT FRAPPE: Take your favorite blended icy drink (be it a smoothie, a milkshake, or yes, even one of those fancy coffee drinks), and serve it in the largest, most ridiculous vessel you can find. We're talking "Big Gulp" size here, people. Bonus points if you can find a drinking horn that big. As you sip your frosty beverage, affecting your best "unbothered Viking" look, casually mention to anyone within earshot, "Ah, yes, 'tis as cold as a frost giant's... well, you know."

For those who prefer their drinks a little stronger, I give you **THOR'S THUNDERBOLT TEA:** Start with a base of strong black tea (English Breakfast works well), then add a shot of spiced rum for a lightning strike of flavor. Serve it piping hot in a sturdy mug. For full effect, slam your mug down on the table after each sip, letting out a satisfied "Ahh!" as if you've just defeated a particularly troublesome frost giant.

And for our teetotaling Vikings, fear not! The **VOLVA'S VISION** is here to satisfy. Mix equal parts pomegranate juice and sparkling water, add a splash of lime juice, and garnish with fresh mint leaves. The deep red color is perfect for channeling your inner Norse seer. Stare deeply into your drink before each sip, as if divining the future. If anyone asks what you see, just mutter something cryptic like, "Storms approach from the east... or maybe I just need to clean my glasses."

Now, no Viking feast would be complete without a show-stopping centerpiece. So let me introduce you to the pièce de résistance of our modern Viking menu.

THE RAGNAROK ROAST.

Picture a massive hunk of meat (beef, pork, lamb – choose your fighter) slow-cooked to perfection, so tender it practically falls apart at the mere mention of Odin's name. But here's where it gets interesting. As the roast cooks, you'll baste it with a glaze made from a reduction of cola (yes, you read that right) mixed with your favorite BBQ sauce. The sugars in the cola caramelize as the roast cooks, creating a sweet and sticky outer layer that's absolutely divine.

When it's time to serve, don't just plonk it on a plate like some common feast. Oh, no. You'll want to present this masterpiece with all the drama it deserves. Place the roast on your largest wooden cutting board (or a shield, if you happen to have one lying around). Surround it with roasted root vegetables – carrots, parsnips, and potatoes – arranged to look like the roots of Yggdrasil stretching out across your table.

Now for the theatrical finale. As your wide-eyed dinner guests watch in anticipation, approach the roast with your meat cleaver held high. In your most dramatic voice, proclaim, "Behold, the Ragnarök Roast! May its flavor be the last thing we taste before the world ends!" Then bring the cleaver down with a satisfying thwack, cleaving the roast in two.

If you've done it right, your guests will burst into spontaneous applause. If you've done it wrong, well... you might want to have the number of a good cleaning service on hand. Either way, it'll be a meal to remember.

But a true Viking feast isn't just about the food – it's about the experience. So, let's talk about how to set the mood for your Norse-inspired nosh-up.

First, the ambiance. Dim the lights and break out every candle you own. (If you don't own any candles, first of all, what kind of Viking are you? And secondly, go buy some candles. I'll wait.) The flickering flames will create the perfect atmosphere, reminiscent of a great mead hall. Just try not to set your beard on fire – nothing ruins a feast quite like the smell of singed facial hair.

Next, the music. Now, I know you're tempted to blast some heavy metal – and hey, I'm not here to judge. But for a truly authentic experience, why not create a playlist of traditional Norse music? The haunting sounds of War Druna or Heilung playing softly in the background will transport you and your guests to the fjords of old. Just be prepared for the occasional urge to grab your imaginary sword and go raiding.

Now, seating arrangements. Forget your fancy dining room table. True Vikings feast communally! Push all your furniture to the walls and lay out some furs on the floor. (No furs? A few strategically placed shag rugs will do in a pinch.) Gather around in a circle, with the food laid out in the center. This arrangement encourages sharing, storytelling, and the occasional playful food fight. Just maybe put a tarp down first if you're particularly worried about your security deposit.

Speaking of storytelling, no Viking feast is complete without some epic tales. Designate a skald (storyteller) for the evening. Their job is to regale the group with stories of great battles, cunning tricks, and godly interventions. Don't know any Norse myths? No problem! Simply recount the plot of the last Marvel movie you watched but replace all the character names with Norse gods. Trust me, after a few horns of mead (or Frost Giant Frappés), no one will know the difference.

And let's not forget about toasts! In Viking culture, toasts were a big deal. So, before each course, stand up (if you can – remember, we're sitting on the floor here), raise your drinking vessel high, and make a toast. Start with the traditional "Skål!" but feel free to get creative. "May your axes always be sharp and your Wi-Fi signal strong!" is a personal favorite.

Now, I know what you're thinking. "This all sounds great, but what about table manners? Didn't Vikings just eat with their hands and throw bones on the floor?" Well, yes and no. While Vikings did have a reputation for being a bit... let's say, boisterous... in their dining habits, that doesn't mean we need to completely abandon modern etiquette. So here are a few rules for modern Viking dining.

1.   It's perfectly acceptable to eat with your hands but maybe keep some wet wipes nearby. Don't be "uncivilized" with greasy fingerprints all over your PlayStation controller.

2.   Feel free to tear into your food with gusto but try not to actually growl at it. Your neighbors might call animal control.

3.   If you must throw something, make it something soft. A dinner roll makes a much better projectile than a chicken bone, and it's less likely to break your TV.

4.   Belching is allowed, nay, encouraged! But maybe save the really impressive ones for after the meal. You don't want to put anyone off their Yggdrasil Salad.

5.   It's customary to compliment the cook. But instead of a simple "Thanks, this is delicious," try something more Viking-appropriate. "By Odin's beard, this feast is worthy of Valhalla itself!" should do the trick.

Remember, the key to a successful Viking feast is enthusiasm. Attack your meal with the same fervor you'd attack a rival clan (metaphorically speaking, of course). Let out the occasional war cry. Bang your fist on the table for emphasis when making a particularly good point in conversation. Get fully into character!

But what about dessert, you ask? Fear not, for I have not forgotten the sweetest part of our feast.

Let me introduce you to the **THOR'S HAMMER SUNDAE:** Start with a base of your favorite ice cream. Vanilla works well, but if you're feeling adventurous, try cardamom or honey flavor for a more Norse-inspired twist. Now, here's where it gets fun. Take two rectangular ice cream sandwiches and stick them together to form the handle of Thor's hammer. Place this "handle" on your plate, then scoop a generous amount of ice cream at one end to form the head of the hammer.

But we're not done yet! Drizzle the whole thing with a caramel sauce (or honey if you're going for historical accuracy). Then sprinkle it with crushed nuts and edible silver sprinkles to make it look appropriately godly. For the final addition, stick a sparkler in the top (if it's legal in your area, of course – we don't want to anger the authorities, Viking-style or not).

When it's time to serve, light the sparkler and present the sundae with a flourish, proclaiming, "Behold, the might of Thor's sweet tooth!" Encourage your guests to eat it quickly before it melts into Bifrost Bridge.

Now, as the feast winds down, and you all sit back, bellies full and spirits high, it's time for one last Viking tradition—the food coma nap. In Norse mythology, Odin is often depicted seated on his throne, Hlidskjalf, from which he can see all the realms. In your case, your throne might be your favorite recliner or that comfy spot on the couch. As you settle in, food belly protruding proudly, you can look out over the remnants of your feast and feel a sense of pride. You have eaten like a Norse god, and now you shall rest like one.

But before you drift off into dreams of Valhalla (or just really vivid food dreams – it could go either way), take a moment to appreciate what you've accomplished. You've turned a simple meal into an epic saga. You've brought a touch of Viking spirit to your modern life. And most importantly, you've created memories that will last... well, at least until your next feast.

So, there you have it, my hungry Viking friends. You now have all the tools you need to feast like a Norse god. Remember, it's not just about the food – it's about the experience, the camaraderie, and the sheer joy of embracing your inner Viking.

Now, if you'll excuse me, all this talk of feasting has made me hungry. I think it's time for me to go raid my own fridge. Skål!

CHAPTER 4

VIKING ETIQUETTE: HOW NOT TO GET YOURSELF EXILED

Picture this: You've mastered the art of the Viking workout, you've feasted like Odin himself, and you're feeling rather good about your newfound Norse identity. Your beard is on point, your mead horn is always full, and you've perfected your war cry to the point where it only slightly alarms your neighbors. You're ready to take on the world, Viking style.

But wait! Before you go charging into your next social gathering like a berserker into battle, we need to talk about something crucial—Viking etiquette. Now, I know what you're thinking. "Etiquette? Vikings? Aren't those mutually exclusive?" Well, my axe-wielding amigo, you might be surprised to learn that even the most fearsome warriors of the North had their own code of conduct. If you want to avoid being metaphorically exiled to the coldest, most remote island in your social circle, you'd do well to learn it.

So, strap on your horned helmet (which, as we've established, isn't historically exact, but looks cool for parties), and let's dive into the fine art of not making a complete fool of yourself in Viking society. Or, you know, at your next themed dinner party.

First things first. Let's talk about axe placement at the dinner table. Now, in our modern world, this might seem like a non-issue. After all, how often do you bring an axe to dinner? But for a Viking, an axe was like a smartphone – you never left home without it. So, where do you put this essential accessory when you're sitting down to feast?

The answer, my friend, is not "buried in the table to prove a point." I don't care how much that guy at the end of the table is bragging about his latest raid – embedding your axe in the wood is considered poor form. Not to mention, it's hell on the finish. Instead, your axe should be placed discreetly under the table, within easy reach in case of surprise attacks or particularly tough cuts of meat.

But what if you're at a modern dinner party and don't actually have an axe? Fear not! The same principle applies to your phone. Keep it under the table, on silent, ready to be whipped out at a moment's notice to settle debates about Norse mythology or to show off pictures of your latest Viking-inspired DIY project. Just try not to get mead on it – those things aren't as waterproof as a good battle axe.

Now, let's move on to a topic dear to every Viking's heart (and face)…the art of the subtle beard brag. In Viking society, a magnificent beard was a sign of wisdom, strength, and the ability to keep small woodland creatures warm in winter. But how do you let everyone know just how impressive your facial hair is without coming across as, well, a bit of a Loki?

The key, my hirsute friend, is subtlety. You can't just walk into the mead hall (or your local coffee shop) and shout, "Behold my glorious face forest!" Well, you can, but don't be surprised if you get some strange looks and possibly a lifetime ban from Starbucks. Instead, try these subtle techniques to draw attention to your magnificent beard.

1. **The thoughtful stroke:** While engaged in conversation, gently stroke your beard as if deep in thought. This draws the eye to your facial hair while also making you look contemplative and wise. Win-win!

2. **The accidental braid:** "Oh, this? I just absentmindedly braided my beard while reading the entire works of Snorri Sturluson. No big deal."

3. **The food save:** When eating, deliberately get a small piece of food stuck in your beard. Then, with the casual air of someone who does this all the time, retrieve it and pop it in your mouth. "Ah, saving this morsel for later. A Viking is always prepared."

4. **The wind catch:** On a breezy day, position yourself so that your beard majestically flows in the wind. Bonus points if you can time it with a dramatic statement or entrance.

Remember, the goal is to make your beard-bragging seem effortless and unintentional. You're not showing off; you're simply existing with an exceptional beard. It's not your fault if people can't help but notice and admire it, right?

But what if you can't grow a beard? Maybe you're follicly challenged, or perhaps you're one of our shield-maiden readers. Fear not! The art of the subtle brag applies to all aspects of Viking life. Maybe you casually mention how you single-handedly moved your couch while cleaning underneath it. Or perhaps you offhandedly refer to the time you ate an entire large pizza by yourself after a particularly grueling "raid" (aka a tough day at the office). The key is to make it seem like these feats of strength and endurance are just everyday occurrences for you.

Now, let's address a topic that might seem at odds with the popular image of Vikings...using your indoor voice in the mead hall. Yes, you read that right. Contrary to what Hollywood would have you believe, Vikings didn't spend all their time shouting at each other over flagons of mead. There's a time and place for your mighty war cry, and surprisingly, it's not "always" and "everywhere."

Think of the mead hall as the Viking equivalent of a trendy gastropub. It's a place for socializing, networking, and maybe bragging about your latest raid (or, in modern terms, your recent promotion or successful Etsy shop launch). But if you're bellowing every word like you're trying to be heard over a battle, you're going to come across less like a respected warrior and more like that one guy at the bar that everyone avoids eye contact with.

So, when should you use your indoor voice? Here's a handy guide.

1. **When regaling your friends with tales of your exploits:** Use a conversational tone. Save the shouting for the really exciting parts, like when you single-handedly fought off a bear (or that time you successfully assembled IKEA furniture without any leftover pieces).

2. **When ordering another round of mead:** The serving staff will appreciate not having their eardrums shattered. Plus, you're less likely to end up with ale when you wanted mead.

3. **When discussing sensitive information:** Maybe you're planning a raid on a nearby village (or just organizing a surprise party for a friend). Either way, keeping your voice down prevents your plans from being overheard by potential enemies or the guest of honor.

4. **When paying a compliment:** "YOUR BEARD LOOKS MAGNIFICENT TODAY, BJORN!" is less a compliment and more an auditory assault.

5. **When flirting:** Trust me, your crush is more likely to be wooed by a smooth, confident murmur than by you

47

shouting pickup lines across the mead hall. Of course, there are times when it's entirely appropriate, nay, expected, to let your inner Viking volume loose.

6. **When toasting:** A hearty "Skål!" should be loud enough to rattle the rafters.

7. **When cheering on your friends in a strength contest:** Whether it's an arm-wrestling match or a heated game of Jenga, feel free to yell encouragement at the top of your lungs.

8. **When singing traditional Viking songs:** If you're not loud enough to wake the gods, are you even trying?

9. **When an enemy raiding party crashes your feast:** This is the perfect time to unleash your war cry. (Note: If this happens at your local bar, maybe just call the bouncer instead.)

Now, let's talk about another crucial aspect of Viking etiquette: the art of the boast. In Viking culture, boasting wasn't just accepted; it was expected. But there's a fine line between impressive boasting and coming across as, well, a bit of a draugr (that's Old Norse for an undead nuisance, in case you were wondering).

The key to a good boast is to make it just believable enough that people want to believe it, even if they're quite sure you're exaggerating. For example:

Good boast: "I once rowed across the fjord in a storm to deliver a message to the next village."

Bad boast: "I once swam across the Atlantic Ocean. Twice. In one day."

See the difference? One is impressive but plausible, while the other is just asking for eye rolls and possibly a one-way ticket to Exileville. In our modern context, the art of the boast might translate to something like this:

Good modern boast: "I managed to get through all my emails and still had time for a Viking workout yesterday."

Bad modern boast: "I answered every email ever sent, reprogrammed the internet to work twice as fast, and still had time to build a longship in my backyard."

Remember, the goal is to impress, not to make people question your grasp on reality.

Now, let's address one of the most important aspects of Viking etiquette: gift-giving. In Norse culture, the exchange of gifts was a crucial part of maintaining social bonds and alliances. But before you start wrapping up your spare battle axe to give to your boss for Secret Santa, let's talk about appropriate gifts in both Viking and modern contexts.

In Viking times, typical gifts might include:

1. **Weapons:** Few things capture, "I value our friendship" like an artfully crafted sword.

2. **Jewelry:** Preferably looted from a successful raid.

3. **Livestock:** Because who doesn't want a goat?

4. **Land:** For when you really want to impress.

In our modern world, you might want to adjust these slightly:

1. A **high-quality kitchen knife set** (all the danger of gifting weapons with none of the legal issues).

2. **Artisanal mead or craft beer** (because some traditions are worth keeping).

49

3. A **houseplant:** It's like livestock, but less messy.

4. A **gift card:** The modern equivalent of gifting land – it's basically giving currency to be exchanged for goods and services.

Remember, in both Viking and modern times, it's not just about the gift itself, but the thought and effort behind it. A well-chosen gift can strengthen bonds, smooth over disagreements, and maybe even prevent you from being challenged to a holmgang (that's a formal duel, for you, non-Viking types).

Speaking of disagreements, let's talk about the Viking approach to conflict resolution. Contrary to trendy belief, Vikings didn't solve every problem with an axe to the face. They had a complex legal system and often settled disputes through discussion and negotiation. Of course, if that failed, then it might come down to a duel, but let's focus on the peaceful methods first.

In Viking society, many conflicts were resolved at the Thing, a regular assembly where legal and political issues were discussed. Think of it as a cross between a court of law and a town hall meeting, but with more beards and axes.

In our modern context, you probably can't call a Thing every time you have a disagreement with a coworker or neighbor. But you can apply some Viking-inspired conflict resolution techniques.

The diplomatic approach: Before resorting to violence (or passive-aggressive sticky notes), try talking it out. Vikings valued clear, direct communication. So, channel your inner Norse negotiator and address the issue head-on.

The compensation offer: In Viking times, many conflicts were resolved through the payment of weregild, a form of compensation. In modern terms, this might translate to offering to buy your neighbor a six-pack as an apology for your noisy Viking rock band practice.

The neutral party mediation: Vikings often called on respected members of the community to mediate disputes. In your case, this might mean asking a mutual friend to help settle an argument or going through HR if it's a workplace issue.

The oath-taking: Vikings placed significant importance on oaths. If you reach an agreement, consider formalizing it with a ceremonial oath. Maybe don't swear on your axe in the break room, but a firm handshake and a clear verbal agreement can work wonders.

The last resort – the Holmgang: If all else fails, you could challenge your opponent to a duel. In modern times, this is best translated to a competitive but friendly contest. Maybe a game of chess, a race, or a bake-off. (Note: Please do not actually challenge people to physical duels. We live in a society, people.)

Now, let's address one final aspect of Viking etiquette that's often overlooked—personal hygiene. Yes, you read that right. Despite their reputation as savage warriors, Vikings were actually quite concerned with cleanliness. Archaeological evidence suggests they bathed regularly, groomed their hair and beards, and even used ear cleaners.

So, if you really want to live like a Viking, put down the "eau de unwashed raider" cologne and pick up some soap. Here are some Viking-inspired grooming tips for the modern world.

1. **Bathe regularly:** Vikings typically bathed once a week, which was frequent for their time. In our modern world, daily showers are more the norm. Think of it as preparing for Ragnarök every day.

2. **Groom that beard:** A well-maintained beard was a point of pride for Vikings. Invest in some good beard

oil and a sturdy comb. Your facial hair should strike fear into the hearts of your enemies, not small children, and health inspectors.

3.   **Take care of your teeth:** Vikings used twigs as makeshift toothbrushes. You have access to modern dental care, so use it! Nothing ruins a fearsome war cry quite like tooth decay.

4.   **Maintain your hair:** Whether you're sporting long locks or a shaved head with an intricate braid design, keep it clean and well-groomed. You want to look like you just stepped off a longship, not like you've been living under one.

5.   **Use deodorant:** This one's not strictly Viking, but trust me, your colleagues at the office will appreciate it. Think of it as a modern version of burning sage to ward off evil spirits. In this case, the evil spirit is your own body odor.

Remember, a clean Viking is a happy Viking. And a happy Viking is less likely to go berserk and alienate all their friends and neighbors.

So, there you have it, my soon-to-be-well-mannered Viking friends. You're now armed with all the knowledge you need to navigate the treacherous waters of Norse social norms without getting yourself exiled (or uninvited from future game nights). Remember, being a Viking isn't just about looking fierce and drinking mead. It's about carrying yourself with the confidence of someone who could totally win a rap battle against Odin himself (not that we recommend challenging the Allfather to a rap battle, mind you).

Now go forth and Viking responsibly! May your axes always be sharp, your beards always be lustrous, and your indoor voices be used appropriately.

CHAPTER 5

HYGIENE: STAYING FRESH ON THE FJORDS

Alright, my soon-to-be-squeaky-clean shield-siblings, it's time to address a topic that might come as a shock to some of you—Viking hygiene. Now, I know what you're thinking. "Hygiene? Vikings? Aren't those two words as incompatible as Loki and trustworthiness?" Well, prepare to have your mind blown like Thor's hammer on a frost giant's noggin because Vikings were actually pretty darn clean for their time.

That's right, contrary to widespread belief, Vikings weren't just a bunch of smelly, unwashed barbarians. In fact, they were known for their cleanliness compared to many of their European contemporaries. Archaeology has uncovered a treasure trove of grooming tools in Viking settlements, from combs to ear spoons (yes, that was a thing), suggesting that these fierce warriors took their personal hygiene seriously.

So, if you want to truly embrace the Viking lifestyle, it's time to ditch the "eau de week-old battle sweat" and learn how to stay fresh, even when you're raiding... Er, I mean, commuting to work on a packed subway train. Let's dive into the world of Norse cleanliness, shall we?

First up on our journey to Viking freshness: organic beard oils and their raiding applications. Now, in the world of the Vikings, a beard wasn't just facial hair – it was a statement. It said, "I am a man of wisdom, strength, and the ability to store snacks for later." But a great beard requires great care, and that's where beard oil comes in.

In Viking times, beard oil might have been made from animal fats or plant oils. Today, we have the luxury of choosing from a wide variety of organic, artisanal beard oils. But why stop at just making your beard soft and shiny? Let's explore some alternative uses that would make any Viking proud.

1. **Emergency lamp fuel:** Your raiding party's torch gone out? No problem! A few drops of your lavender-scented beard oil on a rag, and you're back in business. Not much yells "fearsome warrior" quite like pillaging by the soft glow of aromatherapy.

2. **Weapon lubricant:** Axe getting a bit squeaky? A dab of beard oil will have it swinging smoothly in no time. Plus, your enemies will be too busy wondering why your weapon smells like a spa instead of defending themselves properly.

3. **Fire starter:** In a survival situation, that beard oil could be the difference between a chilly night and a cozy campfire. Just be careful not to accidentally ignite your beard in the process. A flaming beard may look epic, but it's hell on the follicles.

4. **Impromptu massage oil:** After a long day of raiding and pillaging (or you know, answering emails and attending meetings), nothing beats a good shoulder rub. Your beard oil can double as massage oil in a pinch. Just maybe wash your hands before reapplying

it to your face. Nobody wants a beard that smells like feet.

5. **Viking hair gel:** Got a few flyaways in your braids? A touch of beard oil can tame those unruly strands. You'll be the envy of all the other Vikings with your sleek, perfectly styled raid 'do.

Remember, a well-oiled beard is a happy beard. And a happy beard makes for a happy Viking. Just maybe don't mention to your beard oil supplier all the alternative uses you've found for their product. Some things are best kept between you and your facial hair.

Now, let's move on to a topic that might seem more at home in a sci-fi convention than a Viking history book—the hot tub time machine. No, I'm not talking about the movie (although if Vikings had access to time travel, history would be a lot more interesting). I'm talking about the Norse tradition of communal bathing, or as I like to call it, "The Art of the Nordic Spa."

You see, Vikings were big fans of what they called "bath houses." These weren't your modern-day luxury spas with cucumber water and heated towel racks. Oh, no. These were more like... well, imagine a sauna had a baby with a very warm, very crowded swimming pool. That's pretty much what we're dealing with here.

In some Viking settlements, these bath houses were simple affairs – a hole dug in the ground, filled with water, and heated with hot stones. In others, they were more elaborate structures with wooden tubs and even primitive steam rooms. But regardless of the setup, the principle was the same: get naked, get in the water, and get clean. Do this all while surrounded by your fellow Vikings. Hope you're not shy!

Now, I know what you're thinking. "But I don't have access to a Viking bath house! How am I supposed to experience this crucial part of Norse culture?" Fear not, my hygiene-hungry friend. With a little creativity, you too can turn your bathing routine into a Nordic spa experience. Here's how.

1. **The neighbor's pool plunge:** If you're lucky enough to have a neighbor with a pool, congratulations! You're halfway to Viking bathing nirvana. Now, all you need to do is convince said neighbor to let you and all your friends use their pool... in the middle of winter... while you're all naked. Good luck with that conversation!

LEGAL DISCLAIMER

We do not actually recommend trespassing in your neighbor's pool. That's a quick way to get exiled from the neighborhood, Viking-style.

---

2. **The bathroom sauna:** No pool? No problem! Turn your bathroom into a makeshift sauna. Run the shower on the hottest setting, close all the doors and windows, and voilà! Instant steam room. Just be prepared for some awkward explanations when your roommates or family members wonder why you're emerging from the bathroom looking like a lobster and smelling like a Viking warrior.

3. **The backyard hot tub:** If you're feeling really ambitious (and have some carpentry skills), why not build your own Nordic-style hot tub in your backyard? All you need is a large wooden barrel, a way to heat the water, and a complete disregard for your water bill. Invite your friends over for a Viking spa day. Just maybe warn the neighbors first. The sight of a bunch of people in horned helmets (historically inaccurate, but fun) sitting in a barrel in the backyard might be a bit alarming.

4. **The public pool Viking invasion:** If all else fails, there's always the public pool. Now, I'm not suggesting you actually try to recreate a full Viking bath house

experience here. That's a quick way to get banned for life. But you can channel your inner Norse spirit by doing some vigorous lap swimming (pretend you're rowing a longship), followed by some time in the sauna (if available). Just try to resist the urge to belt out Viking war chants in the echoing tiled room. Again, that's how you get banned.

Remember, the key to the Nordic spa experience isn't just about getting clean. It's about community, relaxation, and emerging from the water feeling like you've been reborn as a warrior ready to take on the world (or at least ready to take on the rest of your day without falling asleep at your desk).

Now, let's move on to a topic that's sure to make your head spin: gnarly braids, your hair's passport to Valhalla. In Viking culture, hair wasn't just something that grew on your head. It was a statement, a work of art, and sometimes even a status symbol. Both men and women in Viking society often wore elaborate hairstyles, with braids being particularly popular.

But we're not talking about your basic three-strand braid here. Oh, no. Viking braids were complex, intricate, and often incorporated beads, threads, or even gold wire for the particularly fancy raiders. These weren't just hairstyles. They were wearable art that told a story about who you were and where you came from.

So, how can you incorporate this Viking hair art into your modern life? Well, unless you work in a highly creative field, showing up to the office with a head full of warrior braids might raise a few eyebrows. But fear not! Here are some ways to channel your inner Viking hairstylist without getting called into HR.

1. **The subtle side braid:** Start small with a single braid along one side of your head. It's like a little nod to your Norse ancestors that says, "I could totally raid a village if I wanted to, but I've got this quarterly report to finish first."

2. **The weekend warrior:** Save your more elaborate styles for the weekend. Nothing states, "I'm ready for a modern-day raid" quite like showing up to brunch with a head full of intricate braids. Your friends will be too busy trying to figure out how you did it to notice you stealing bites of their avocado toast.

3. **The gym Viking:** Braids are fantastic for keeping hair out of your face during a workout. Channel your inner shield-maiden with some fierce braids at the gym. Who knows, it might even improve your battle... Er, I mean, deadlift technique.

4. **The special occasion Odin:** Got a big event coming up? Why not go all out with a full Viking-inspired hairstyle? Weddings, Renaissance fairs, or Viking metal concerts are all perfect opportunities to let your Norse flag fly, follicle-wise.

5. **The bearded braid:** And let's not forget about facial hair! If you're sporting a magnificent Viking beard, why not incorporate some small braids into it? Showing up with a braided beard in a board meeting says, "I mean business".

You might be thinking, "But I can barely manage a ponytail, let alone some complex Viking braid!" Fear not, my follicly challenged friend. The Vikings had a solution for that too. Many Viking men who were losing their hair would grow it long at the back and sides, creating an early version of the "skillet" (that's skull + mullet, for the uninitiated). So, embrace your baldness like a true Norse warrior!

Remember, the key to Viking hair isn't just the style – it's the attitude. Whether you're rocking a head full of intricate braids or proudly sporting a shiny dome, wear it with the confidence of someone who could totally steal a monastery's entire supply of illuminated manuscripts (but chooses not to because that would be wrong, and also where would you store them in your tiny apartment?).

Now, let's address the elephant in the room – or should I say, the bilgesnipe in the bath house. How do you maintain all this Viking cleanliness when you're you know, actually living like a Viking? When you're out on a longship for weeks at a time, raiding monasteries and exploring new lands, it's not like you can just pop into a lush store for some artisanal soap.

Well, my resourceful raider, the Vikings had solutions for that too. They were masters of using what nature provided to keep themselves (relatively) fresh and clean. Here are some Viking-approved hygiene hacks for when you're roughing it.

1. **Sea foam shampoo:** Why buy expensive shampoo when the ocean provides? A good scrub with some sea foam was a Viking's version of a 2-in-1 shampoo and conditioner. Plus, the salt in the water acted as a natural styling product. Talk about beach waves!

2. **Sand scrub:** No loofah? No problem! A handful of sand makes for an excellent exfoliant. Just be careful not to scrub too hard. You want to emerge from your bath looking fresh and Viking-y, not like you've been attacked by an incredibly determined cat.

3. **Birch leaf deodorant:** Vikings would use birch leaves as a natural deodorant. Simply crush the leaves and apply to your underarms. You'll smell fresh and forest, like a Viking who's just pillaged a particularly aromatic grove.

4. **Urine as mouthwash:** Okay, this one's a bit gross, but hey, when in Rome (or Scandinavia) ... Vikings would sometimes use urine as a mouthwash due to its antibacterial properties. Maybe stick to modern mouthwash for this one. Your breath, and your friends, will thank you.

5. **Ear spoons:** These were exactly what they sound like
    – tiny spoons for cleaning your ears. You will be,
    "ready for battle" quite like meticulously clean ear
    canals.

Remember, hygiene isn't just about smelling nice (although
that's certainly a bonus, especially in close quarters on a
longship). It's about health, self-respect, and being prepared for
whatever Odin might throw your way. Whether you're facing
down a horde of angry Anglo-Saxons or just a particularly
grueling day at the office, you'll face it better when you're fresh
and clean.

So, there you have it, my squeaky-clean shield-siblings.
You're now armed with all the knowledge you need to stay fresh,
even when you're conquering new lands (or just conquering
your to-do list). Remember, a clean Viking is a happy Viking.
And a happy Viking is a Viking who's ready to take on the
world, one well-groomed raid at a time.

Now, if you'll excuse me, all this talk of cleanliness has
made me want to go oil my beard and braid my... well, whatever
hair I have left.

CHAPTER 6

VIKING CHIC: DRESSING TO OPPRESS

Alright, my fashion-forward fjord-dwellers, it's time to talk about the most important aspect of any aspiring Viking's life: your wardrobe. Now, I know what you're thinking. "Vikings? Fashion? Aren't those two words about as compatible as Loki and honesty?" But hold on to your horned helmets (which, as we've established, aren't historically accurate, but look cool) because you're about to discover that Vikings were the original influencers of the medieval world.

That's right, long before Instagram models and fashion bloggers, Vikings were setting trends across Europe. They were the OG style icons, raiding not just for gold and silver, but for the latest in Anglo-Saxon and Frankish fashion. These seafaring fashionistas were known for their love of bright colors, intricate patterns, and enough bling to make a rapper blush.

So, if you want to truly embrace the Viking lifestyle, it's time to raid your own wardrobe and pillage the local shopping mall. But fear not, my budget-conscious berserker, for we have a secret weapon in our quest for Viking chic: eBay, the digital marketplace that's as vast and full of treasures as Odin's own halls.

Let's start with the cornerstone of any Viking wardrobe: furs. Now, in the days of old, Vikings would hunt their own furs or trade for them. But unless you're prepared to chase down a bear with nothing but a pointy stick and your own Viking moxie (please don't actually do this), we're going to have to find an alternative. Enter the wonderful world of polyester furs on eBay.

Ah, polyester! The fabric of the gods (if the gods shopped at discount stores). It's durable, it's washable, and best of all, no animals were harmed in its making. Perfect for the ethically minded marauder. But how do you find the cream of the crop in the vast sea of eBay listings? Here are some tips for scoring the most authentic-looking polyester furs.

1. **Search smart:** Don't just type in "Viking fur." Get creative with your keywords. Try "faux fur vest," "medieval cloak," or "Game of Thrones cosplay" for some surprising finds.

2. **Check the reviews:** If a seller's furs have been described as "looking like roadkill" or "shedding worse than my cat," maybe give that one a miss.

3. **Zoom in:** Use the zoom function to check the quality of the fur. If it looks like it might be made from the stuffing of a 1970s sofa, keep scrolling.

4. **Ask questions:** Don't be afraid to message the seller. "How many mead stains can this fur hide?" is a perfectly reasonable question for a Viking to ask.

5. **Bundle and save:** Many eBay sellers offer discounts if you buy multiple items. Why stop at one fur when you can have a whole collection? Variety is the spice of Viking life, after all.

Remember, the key to rocking polyester fur is confidence. Stride into your local coffee shop wearing your new eBay-sourced fur vest, order your venti triple-shot oat milk latte with the authority of someone who just pillaged three villages before breakfast, and dare anyone to question your fashion choices.

But furs are just the beginning of your Viking fashion journey. Let's talk about accessories, specifically, how to accessorize your battle axe for casual Fridays. Now, I know what you're thinking. "Casual Fridays? Battle axes? Am I going to get fired?" Don't worry, my employment-concerned einherjar. With a little creativity, you can incorporate your warrior spirit into your office attire without setting off any HR alarms.

First things first. Unless you work at a very understanding Renaissance faire, you probably can't bring an actual battle axe to the office. But who says you can't have an axe-inspired accessory? Here are some ideas.

1. **The axe tie clip:** It screams, "I'm ready for that quarterly report and also Ragnarök follower" with a miniature axe holding your tie in place.

2. **Battle axe cufflinks:** For when you need to bring a touch of Viking flair to your suit and tie ensemble.

3. **Axe-shaped pen:** Perfect for signing important documents or dramatically pointing at pie charts during presentations.

4. **Viking-inspired briefcase:** Who needs a boring old leather briefcase when you can have one shaped like a shield? Bonus points if it has an axe design embossed on it.

5. **Axe body spray:** Okay, this one's a bit on the nose (literally), but sometimes you've got to commit to the bit. Just maybe go easy on the application. You want

to smell like a warrior, not a middle school locker room.

Remember, the key to casual Friday Viking style is subtlety. You're going for "culturally aware professional with a quirky side," not "time-traveling berserker who's confused about where he is."

Now, let's address a fashion emergency that every modern Viking has faced at some point—how to explain your chainmail rash to your doctor. Imagine that you've been rocking your authentic(ish) chainmail shirt all weekend at the Viking reenactment festival. You felt like a true warrior, but now your skin looks like you've cuddled with a cheese grater. What do you do?

First of all, kudos on your commitment to historical accuracy. Secondly, here are some tips for that awkward doctor's visit.

1. **Be honest... ish:** "I have a bit of a rash from some new workout gear" is technically true and much less likely to get you a psych evaluation than "I got this from wearing chainmail while pretending to pillage my neighbor's herb garden."

2. **Blame it on cosplay:** In this era of superhero movies and fantasy TV shows, saying "It's a cosplay thing" can explain away a multitude of sins.

3. **The allergic reaction excuse:** "I think I'm allergic to my new shirt" is not too far from the truth. You are, in fact, allergic to wearing metal armor without proper padding.

4. **The DIY project gone wrong:** "I was trying out a new craft project with metal rings" is vague enough to be believable but specific enough to explain the pattern of your rash.

5. **Embrace the truth:** If all else fails, own it. Look your doctor in the eye and say, "I was wearing chainmail because I'm embracing my inner Viking." Who knows? Maybe your doctor is secretly longing to join a Norse reenactment society too.

Remember, whatever explanation you choose, follow your doctor's advice for treating the rash. Even the mightiest Viking warriors need to take care of their skin.

Now, let's circle back to eBay, that digital Bifrost bridge connecting us mere mortals to the realm of Viking fashion. We've covered furs, but there's so much more to discover in this online treasure trove. eBay isn't just for polyester pelts and questionable antiques. It's a veritable smorgasbord of Viking-inspired fashion finds.

Let's start with the basics: **tunics**. A good tunic is to a Viking what a little black dress is to Audrey Hepburn – timeless, versatile, and always in style. Search for "medieval tunic" or "Viking shirt" on eBay, and you'll find options ranging from historically accurate linen pieces to more... creative interpretations. **Pro tip:** Look for tunics with side slits for ease of movement. You never know when you might need to breakdance... I mean, engage in a sudden sword fight.

Next up: **pants**. Viking pants, or "trousers" if you're feeling fancy, were typically made of wool and rather baggy. On eBay, search for "Viking pants," "medieval trousers," or "harem pants" if you're feeling particularly flowy. Remember, the baggier, the better. You want pants that say, "I'm ready for a feast, a fight, or a spontaneous nap – whatever Odin throws my way."

Don't forget about **footwear**! Viking shoes were typically made of leather and looked a bit like moccasins. Search for "medieval leather shoes" or "Viking boots" on eBay. If you can't find anything authentic looking, a pair of sturdy brown leather boots will do in a pinch. Just try not to get caught up in a bidding war with some overzealous LARPers — those folks play for keeps.

Now, let's talk about the pièce de résistance of any Viking outfit: the **helmet**. Yes, I know we've established that horned helmets aren't historically accurate, but let's be real — they look awesome. Search for "Viking helmet" on eBay, and you'll find everything from realistic replicas to plastic party hats. Choose wisely, my friend. Remember, you're not just buying headgear; you're investing in a conversation starter.

But what if you're folliciley challenged in the facial hair department? Fear not, my smooth-cheeked shield-brother, for eBay has a solution for that too: **fake beards**! That's right, with the magic of spirit gum and synthetic hair, you too can sport a beard that would make Odin himself stroke his chin in admiration.

When shopping for a fake beard on eBay, keep these tips in mind.

1. **Color match:** Try to find a beard that matches your natural hair color. Unless you're going for the "dyed my beard with leftover henna" look, in which case, Viking on, you magnificent weirdo.

2. **Style variety:** Look for beards that come with detachable sections. This way, you can go from "neatly trimmed warrior-poet" to "wild-man of the fjords" with just a few clip-on pieces.

3. **Material matters:** Synthetic hair is fine for occasional wear, but if you're planning on making fake-bearding a regular part of your routine, consider investing in a higher-quality human hair beard. Your skin (and your date) will thank you.

4. **Read the reviews:** Pay special attention to comments about the adhesive. There's nothing worse than your

beard making a bid for freedom halfway through your war cry.

5. **Practice makes perfect:** Once you get your eBay beard, practice putting it on before any big Viking events. You don't want to show up to the mead hall with your beard askew, looking like you've been in a fight with a drunken barber.

Remember, wearing a fake beard is as much about attitude as it is about appearance. Stroke it thoughtfully during meetings. Get food stuck in it at lunch. Dramatically stroke it while dispensing wisdom. Really commit to the beard life.

Now, let's address the elephant in the room – or should I say, the Gjallarhorn in the great hall. How do you incorporate all these Viking fashion elements into your everyday life without looking like you've got lost on your way to a Renaissance faire?

The key, my style-savvy Norseman, is moderation and modern interpretation. Here are some tips for Viking-ifying your wardrobe without going full berserker.

1. **The business Viking:** Trade your suit jacket for a sleek leather vest over your dress shirt. It's like a modern interpretation of Viking armor, but HR-approved.

2. **Casual raider:** Pair your favorite jeans with a flowy, tunic-style shirt. Add a leather cuff bracelet for that subtle warrior touch.

3. **Weekend warrior:** This is where you can really let your inner Viking shine. Baggy linen pants, a chunky knit sweater, and some sturdy boots create a look that says, "I could totally build a longship, but I'd rather just chill with some mead."

4. **Accessory ace:** Sometimes, a small touch is all you need. A Thor's hammer pendant, some runic cufflinks, or a braided leather belt can add a Norse twist to any outfit.

5. **The formal fjord-explorer:** Attending a black-tie event? Why not swap out your boring black bow tie for one with a subtle Viking ship pattern? It's a conversation starter that doesn't scream "I'm wearing a costume!"

Remember, Viking style is as much about attitude as it is about clothing. Wear your eBay-sourced, polyester, fur-trimmed, probably-not-entirely-historically-accurate outfit with the confidence of someone who could navigate a longship through a storm while composing epic poetry.

And if anyone questions your fashion choices? Simply fix them with your most intimidating stare and say, "Odin approves of this outfit." They'll either be impressed by your dedication or too confused to argue. Either way, you win.

Now, as we wrap up our journey through the wild world of Viking fashion, let's take a moment to appreciate how far we've come. From raiding eBay for polyester furs to explaining chainmail rashes to bewildered medical professionals, you've truly embraced the spirit of the Norse fashionista.

Remember, being a modern Viking isn't just about how you look – it's a state of mind. It's about facing the world with the courage of someone who would sail into the unknown on a wooden boat. It's about approaching your daily challenges with the strategic mind of a master raider. And yes, it's about looking damn good while doing it all.

So go forth, my fabulously dressed friend. Stride into your day with the confidence of a Viking striding into battle. Let your polyester fur flutter in the breeze of the office air conditioning. Let your fake beard strike fear into the hearts of your enemies (or at least mildly confuse your coworkers).

And if anyone dares to question your sartorial choices, simply raise your coffee mug high and proclaim, "Skål! This conversation is over" quite like a Norse toast delivered with conviction.

Now, if you'll excuse me, I have an eBay auction for a chain mail necktie to win. A Viking's work in the realm of fashion is never done!

CHAPTER 7

VIKING LIVING – FROM HOME DECOR TO TRAVEL ADVENTURES ON A BUDGET

Welcome back, aspiring Vikings, to our expanded guide on living your best Norse life on a budget. We've pillaged the depths of creativity (and possibly a few garage sales) to bring you even more ideas for transforming your living space, your mode of transportation, and your travel experiences into a Viking saga come to life. So, grab your IKEA allen wrench (the modern Viking's weapon of choice) and let's dive deeper into the world of Viking-inspired living!

PART I: HOME DECOR – VALHALLA ON A BUDGET

THE ART OF RUNIC WALL DECOR

Why settle for boring old motivational posters when you can adorn your walls with mysterious and powerful runes? Not only will they give your home that authentic Viking vibe, but they'll also make for enjoyable conversation starters. Here's how to create your own runic wall art.

1. **Choose your runes wisely.** Maybe avoid ones that translate to "Death to all who enter" for your guest bedroom. Instead, opt for more welcoming phrases like "May mead flow freely" or "Odin's wisdom dwells here." Just be prepared to explain to your non-Viking friends why your walls are covered in what looks like very angular graffiti.

2. **Materials:** You'll need some wooden planks (reclaimed wood for extra Viking points), paint, and a steady hand. If your hand isn't steady, just claim the wobbly lines are part of the "ancient" look. After all, carving runes on a moving longship wasn't exactly conducive to perfect penmanship.

3. **Paint your chosen runes onto the wood.** Remember, the more weathered and mysterious they look, the better. Feel free to add some artful splatters – it could be mead stains or battle scars, depending on your storytelling mood.

4. **Hang your runic creations on the wall.** Bonus points if you arrange them in a way that accidentally summons Thor. (Note: We are not responsible for any thunder gods that may appear in your living room. If one does show up, offer him a Pop-Tart. We hear he's quite fond of them.)

5. For an extra touch of authenticity, consider **adding some "burn" marks around the edges of your rune plaques.** It'll look like they survived a dragon attack, and it's a wonderful way to cover up any mistakes you made while painting!

THE MYTHICAL BEAST THROW PILLOW PROJECT

Every Viking longhouse needs some fearsome beasts, but since keeping a live dragon in your apartment is generally frowned upon (and violates most lease agreements), we'll have to get creative.

1. Find some plain **throw pillows.** The cheap ones from IKEA work great. Consider "Fjällbo" or "Vigdis" for that extra Norse touch.

2. Get some fabric paint and let your inner Viking artist loose. **Paint serpents, dragons, wolves, or any other mythical beast that strikes your fancy.** Remember, in Norse mythology, the scarier, the better. Your couch should look like it could eat unwary visitors at any moment.

3. For the less artistically inclined, find some Norse-inspired **iron-on transfers online.** It's not cheating; it's using your resources wisely, like any good Viking would. Plus, iron-on transfers are basically modern-day rune magic.

4. Don't stop at just one or two pillows. **Cover every soft surface in your home with mythical beasts.** Your couch should look like a menagerie of creatures that would give Loki nightmares.

5. For an interactive touch, **create a giant Jörmungandr (the world serpent) pillow** that wraps around your entire couch. It's decorative and a fantastic way to trap your friends when they come over. "Oh, you want to leave? Sorry, the world serpent has you in its coils. Guess you'll have to stay for another mead!"

6. Don't forget about Fenrir the wolf. **A large, wolf-shaped body pillow** could serve as both decor and a comfy place to nap. Just don't let it near any suspiciously hand-shaped pillows, or you might have to recreate the binding of Fenrir in your living room.

THE MEAD HALL DINING EXPERIENCE

Transform your dining area into a proper Viking mead hall. Your dinner parties will never be the same!

1. **Replace your dining chairs with benches.** If you can't find affordable benches, just remove the backs from your existing chairs. Voilà! Instant mead hall seating. Plus, it makes it much easier to dramatically stand up and deliver boastful speeches about your day's conquests (or your success in finally figuring out the office printer).

2. **Create a centerpiece using a toy Viking longship.** Fill it with flowers, fruit, or mini liquor bottles for that authentic raided village look. For special occasions, set it on fire (safely, please) for a miniature Viking funeral centerpiece. Ahhh "festive dinner party" with a burning ship on your table.

3. **Invest in some drinking horns.** They're actually quite affordable online, and it says "Viking feast" sipping your beverage from a horn. Pro tip: Start with something easy like water or juice before moving on to mead. Drinking from a horn takes practice, and you don't want to christen your new Viking decor with spilled mead.

4. **Hang some fake weaponry on the walls.** Plastic swords and axes can usually be found cheaply at party supply stores. Just be prepared to explain to concerned

visitors that no, you haven't actually raided any villages lately. The broadsword is for cutting pizza, you swear.

5. **Install a "mead fountain" as a centerpiece.** It's like a chocolate fountain, but with mead (or apple juice for the non-drinkers). It's impractical, probably messy, but undeniably Viking.

6. **Don't forget the mood lighting!** Replace your regular light bulbs with flickering LED "flame" bulbs. It's like dining by torchlight, but without the fire hazard.

7. **For the full mead hall experience,** hire a local bard (or a friend with a guitar) to regale your guests with tales of your glorious deeds. If you can't find a willing bard, a dramatic reading of IKEA instruction manuals in a Norse accent works too.

THE BIFROST BATHROOM

Why should your living room have all the fun? Bring some Norse magic into your bathroom with these Bifrost-inspired ideas.

1. **Rainbow shower curtain:** Find a rainbow-striped shower curtain to represent the Bifrost bridge. Every shower becomes a magical journey! Just be careful not to slip — falling off the Bifrost is no joke, even if it's just into your bathtub.

2. **Bifrost bathmat:** Paint a plain bathmat with rainbow stripes. It's like stepping onto the rainbow bridge every time you exit the shower. For extra flair, add some LED lights under a clear mat to make it glow like the real Bifrost.

3. **Heimdall's toothbrush holder:** Find a figurine that looks vaguely like Heimdall (or just a generic Viking warrior) and turn it into a toothbrush holder. Your oral hygiene has never been so well-guarded! You can tell your dentist that Heimdall himself is watching over your teeth.

4. **Rune-inscribed soap dispenser:** Write some Norse runes on your soap dispenser with permanent marker. Washing your hands has never felt so mystical. Choose runes that translate to "Cleanliness is next to Odin-lines's" for that perfect blend of humor and hygiene.

5. **Thor's hammer shower head:** Replace your boring old shower head with one shaped like Mjölnir. Every shower becomes a thunderous experience!

6. **Loki's mirror:** Install a trick mirror that distorts reflections. It's perfect for those "Is this really what I look like?" mornings, and it honors the trickster god himself.

7. **Valkyrie bathrobes:** Upgrade your bathrobe game with a Valkyrie-inspired design. Wings optional but highly recommended for that "fresh from Valhalla" look.

THE YGGDRASIL BOOKSHELF

Turn a plain bookshelf into a representation of Yggdrasil, the world tree. It's functional, educational, and a wonderful way to confuse your non-Viking friends!

1. **Start with a tall, preferably wooden bookshelf.** The BILLY from IKEA works well (of course it does, this is

a budget Viking guide after all). If you're feeling extra crafty, try to find one that's actually tree shaped.

2. **Paint or decal a tree design on the sides and top of the bookshelf.** Don't worry if it's not perfect – Yggdrasil has seen some things; it's allowed to be a bit wonky. Add some fake vines or leaves for extra tree-ness.

Designate each shelf as one of the nine worlds from Norse mythology. You can label them or just organize your books and knick-knacks thematically. Here's a quick guide.

a) **Top shelf (Asgard):** This is where you keep your most impressive books or items. Maybe that copy of "Norse Mythology for Dummies" you've been hiding, or your fanciest mead horn.

b) **Second shelf (Alfheim):** Perfect for your fantasy novels and anything sparkly. Elves love that stuff.

c) **Third shelf (Vanaheim):** Dedicate this to books about nature, fertility, and wisdom. Your gardening books and that self-help book you never finished can go here.

d) **Fourth shelf (Midgard):** This is for your everyday items. Cookbooks, modern fiction, maybe a miniature version of your house.

e) **Fifth shelf (Jotunheim):** Big books go here. Encyclopedias, dictionaries, anything that could be used as a weapon in a pinch.

f) **Sixth shelf (Nidavellir/Svartalfheim):** This is for your craft books, DIY guides, and anything related to metalworking or jewelry. Also, a good spot for your rock collection.

g) **Seventh shelf (Muspelheim):** Red books, spicy cookbooks, and anything related to fire or volcanoes. A lava lamp would not be out of place here.

h) **Eighth shelf (Niflheim):** Cool colors and misty themes reign here. Books about ice and snow, maybe a mini fog machine for effect.

i) **Bottom shelf (Helheim):** This is perfect for those books you bought with good intentions but never actually read. We all have them, no judgment here. Also, a suitable place for gothic literature and murder mysteries.

Don't forget to add some inhabitants to your world tree! Small figurines of Norse gods, giants, and creatures can be placed on appropriate shelves. A stuffed squirrel toy could represent Ratatoskr, the messenger squirrel who runs up and down Yggdrasil.

For an interactive touch, hang a small bucket on a string from the top of the bookcase down to the bottom. This represents the well of Urd at the base of Yggdrasil. Use it to leave notes for your housemates or to store small items.

Lighting is key! String some fairy lights around the bookcase to represent the stars in the Norse cosmos. If you're feeling tech-savvy, set up color-changing LED strips to give each realm its own unique ambiance.

Finally, don't forget the roots. At the base of your Yggdrasil bookshelf, create a small scene representing the three wells: Urd (fate), Verdandi (present), and Skuld (future). This could be as simple as three small bowls with water, or you could go all out with a mini water feature.

Remember, your Yggdrasil bookshelf is not just furniture — it's a conversation piece, a storage solution, and a crash course in Norse mythology all in one!

THE FENRIR FUR RUG FAKE-OUT

Every Viking longhouse needs a majestic fur rug, but since we're modern, ethical Vikings, we'll have to get creative.

1. **Find a large, shaggy bathroom rug**. The shaggier, the better. If you can find one that's already vaguely wolf-shaped, you're halfway there.

2. **Trim it into a wolf-like shape.** Don't worry about perfection — Fenrir was probably a bit scraggly anyway. If you mess up, just say it's a wolf that's been through Ragnarök.

3. **Add felt or fabric eyes and teeth.** The more comically fierce, the better. Remember, Fenrir was supposed to be terrifying, so go big or go home. Glow-in-the-dark paint for the eyes adds a nice touch for nighttime ambiance (or midnight snack runs).

4. For extra authenticity, **attach a felt or fabric chain to represent Gleipnir,** the magical binding that held Fenrir. Bonus points if you can convince your guests, it's the actual mythical chain.

5. **Place your "Fenrir rug" in front of your favorite chair or by the fireplace.** Tell guests it's your loyal wolf, enchanted to guard your home. For fun, record some wolf growls on your phone and play them occasionally to freak out unsuspecting visitors.

6. Don't stop at just one Fenrir! **Create a whole pack of wolf rugs in many sizes.** Scatter them around your home for that "raised by wolves" aesthetic.

7. For the ultimate commitment to the bit, **practice your wolf howl.** Every time you step on your Fenrir rug, let out a mighty "Awoooo!" It's great for scaring away door-to-door salespeople and asserting dominance over your household pets.

THE VALKYRIE VANITY

Who says Vikings can't be glamorous? Turn your vanity or dressing table into a tribute to the Valkyries.

1. **Find some cheap, plastic dollar store shields.** Paint them gold or silver and attach them to the edges of your mirror for a warrior-chic look. Make sure they're securely attached – you don't want to accidentally recreate the crash of the Valkyries.

2. **Replace your regular mirror with a circular one** – it's like looking into Odin's eye! Bonus points if you can find a mirror with a frame that looks like Odin's ravens, Huginn and Muninn.

3. **Use weapon-shaped objects as organizers.** A small axe becomes a ring holder; a sword letter opener can hold your makeup brushes. Just be careful not to grab your actual sword in a pre-coffee morning haze.

4. **Drape some fake ivy or branches around the mirror.** It's not just a vanity; it's a gateway to Fólkvangr! Add some small bird figurines to represent the Valkyries themselves.

5. **Replace your vanity stool with a small wooden chest or barrel.** It's seating and storage in one, perfect for holding your beauty products (or battle trophies, we don't judge).

6. **Hang a small chalkboard nearby to write your daily affirmations in runes.** "Today, I will conquer my to-do list like a Viking raiding party!"

7. **Don't forget the lighting!** Replace your vanity lights with torch-like sconces for that authentic Valkyrie glow. LED flameless candles work great for this and won't set your new ivy decor on fire.

THE NORSE GOD FITNESS CORNER

Who needs a fancy home gym when you can work out like the Norse gods? Create a Viking-inspired fitness corner that Thor himself would be proud of.

1. **Replace your regular dumbbells with a toy Mjölnir.** It may not be as heavy but lifting it still makes you worthy. Plus, it doubles as a great paperweight when you're not working out.

2. **Hang a punching bag** and draw a Jötunn face on it. Nothing motivates a workout like preparing for Ragnarök. Name your Jötunn punching bag for extra motivation. "Take that, Brenda from HR!"

3. **Yoga mat**? You mean your portable Viking ship deck for plank poses. Paint your yoga mat to look like wooden planks for that authentic longship feel. Every downward dog becomes a "Viking pushing longship into water" pose.

4. **Create workout cards** with Norse-inspired names. "Odin's One-Legged Squats," "Thor's Thunder Thrusters," and "Loki's Trickster Twists" should get you started. Don't forget "Sif's Golden Hair Crunches" and "Froya's Chariot Pulls."

5. **Replace your regular jump rope** with a replica of Jörmungandr, the world serpent. Every skip is like leaping over the serpent that encircles Midgard!

6. Set up a **"Viking Obstacle Course"** using household items. Leap over ottomans (mountain ranges), crawl under tables (low cave entrances), and swing from doorways (boarding enemy ships). Just be sure to warn your roommates or family before they walk into your "raid in progress."

7. Don't forget to put up a **poster** of the Norse gods with the caption "Valhalla's Gym: Train Now or Train in the Afterlife." Motivation: Viking style! Add some before and after pictures of Thor. (Before: Scrawny comic book artist Steve. After: Chris Hemsworth) for extra inspiration.

8. **Replace your regular foam roller with a log-shaped one.** It's like rolling on a fallen Yggdrasil branch! Paint it with runes for extra mystical muscle recovery.

9. Invest in a **battle rope** and attach dragon heads to each end. Now you're not just doing rope slams, you're taming mythical beasts with every workout!

10. **Create a "Mead Hall of Fame"** wall where you track your fitness achievements. Did you finally master "Loki's Limbo"? Mark it down! Conquered "Thor's Thousand Thunderclap Pushups"? That deserves a place of honor!

The Ragnarok-Resistant Safe Room

Every modern Viking needs a place to weather the apocalypse. Turn a closet or small room into your own Ragnarök-resistant safe space.

1. Stock it with **non-perishable foods**. Bonus points if they're traditional Norse foods like dried fish and pickled herring. (Your nose may regret this decision, but your taste buds will thank you during the end times.) Don't forget to include a healthy supply of Pop-Tarts – Thor's favorite post-Ragnarök snack.

2. Line the walls with **fake fur or wool blankets** for insulation. It's not just cozy; it's protection against Fimbulwinter! Create a nest-like sleeping area and call it your "Hibernating Dragon's Lair."

3. **Create an "emergency Viking kit"** with essentials like a toy sword, a horned helmet (historically inaccurate, but fun), and a book of Norse mythology. You know, the real essentials. Include a flashlight that you've modified to look like Odin's spear, Gunning.

4. Don't forget a **sign** on the door that says, "Ragnarök Shelter: Midgard's Last Stand." Add a whiteboard to keep track of how many days you've survived the apocalypse. "Day 37: Still no sign of Fenrir. Beginning to suspect the neighbor's chihuahua may be him in disguise."

5. Install a small **fountain or water feature** to represent the Well of Urd. It's decorative and can serve as an emergency water source. Plus, you can pretend to consult it for wisdom during tough times.

6. **Hang a map of the Nine Worlds on the wall.** Use it to plan your post-Ragnarök travel itinerary. "Once the fire giants are dealt with, Muspelheim could be a lovely vacation spot!"

7. Include a variety of **board games and puzzles** to pass the time. Viking chess (Hnefatafl) is a must-have. You could even create your own "Survive Ragnarök" board game!

LOKI'S MISCHIEF CORNER

Every home needs a little chaos. Dedicate a corner of your living space to the trickster god himself.

1. **Hang a mirror with a frame painted to look like snakes.** It's a nod to Loki's children and a terrific way to check if you've got anything in your teeth. Add a small sign that says, "Objects in mirror may be more mischievous than they appear."

2. Place a jar labeled **"Loki's Tricks"** filled with joke items like fake spiders, whoopee cushions, and joy buzzers. Leave it somewhere visitors might be tempted to explore. The real trick? It's actually full of glitter that explodes when opened. Loki would approve.

3. Create a small **"Shapeshifting Station"** with silly disguises like fake mustaches, wigs, and glasses. Loki would approve of spontaneous identity changes. Include a chart showing Loki's various transformations throughout mythology – horse, salmon, fly, etc.

4. Set up a **"Prophecy Prank Phone"** – an old phone that plays recorded "prophecies" when picked up. These can range from ominous Ragnarök warnings to mundane predictions like "You will eat a sandwich today."

5. Don't forget a SIGN that says, "Mischief Managed" – wait, wrong mythology. Make that **"Mischief Encouraged."** Add a scoreboard where you can tally up successful pranks and tricks.

6. Include a small **"Transformation" area** with a curtain. Step behind as yourself, step out as a "different person" (or animal). It's just you with a funny hat on, but hey, Loki started somewhere too!

7. Have a **"Riddle of the Day" board** where you post Norse-themed brain teasers. Example: "I have eight legs, but I'm not a spider. Odin rides me, but I'm not a horse. What am I?" (Answer: Sleipnir, Odin's eight-legged horse... who is actually Loki's child. Norse mythology is wild!)

THE VIKING HOME OFFICE

Working from home? Why not make your home office worthy of a Norse scribe?

1. **Replace your office chair with a throne-like seat.** A folding chair spray-painted gold and draped with a fur throw works in a pinch. Bonus points if you can attach small wooden dragon heads to the armrests.

2. **Upgrade your desk nameplate** to a mini runestone with your name carved (or painted) on it. Add your title too: "Björn the Mighty, Conqueror of Spreadsheets."

3. **Use a drinking horn as a pencil holder**. "I'm ready for that 10 AM meeting," then reach for a pen from a horn. Make sure it's empty though, accidentally drinking last week's coffee is not a wonderful way to start your workday.

4. Frame your diplomas or certificates in **wooden frames carved with Norse knotwork.** Your PhD just got a lot more impressive when it looks like it was bestowed upon you by Odin himself.

5. **Replace your boring mousepad with a circular one painted to look like a Viking shield.** Every spreadsheet becomes a battle! Create a paper-axe letter opener to complete the warrior-scribe aesthetic.

6. Set up a **"Raven Mail"** system. Get two stuffed ravens and place them by your window. Pretend to send messages with them when you need a break from emails. "Huginn, take this message to Karen in accounting. Muninn, fly to the kitchen and see if there's any mead left."

7. Instead of a stress ball, keep a **small plush Jörmungandr (World Serpent)** on your desk. Whenever work gets stressful, give it a squeeze and mutter "Not Ragnarök yet, not Ragnarök yet..."

8. Create a **"Valhalla's Waiting List"** board where you can write down your daily tasks. Crossing them off becomes "sending them to Valhalla." It makes even the most mundane tasks feel epic!

The Freya-Inspired Love Nest

For the romantic Vikings out there, why not create a boudoir that would make Freya proud?

1. String **fairy lights** around your bed frame to represent Freya's famous necklace, Brísingamen. For added effect, hang small jewel-toned glass ornaments among the lights.

2. Place two large **stuffed cats** at the foot of your bed to represent Freya's feline companions. They're guardians of your sleep and much less messy than real cats. Name them and talk to them like Freya would – they're not just decor; they're part of the family!

3.   Hang a **dreamcatcher** made with feathers to represent Freya's falcon cloak. Sweet dreams of flying through Asgard await! Add small charms representing love, beauty, and war (Freya's domains) for extra thematic points.

4.   Create a **"Love Potion" station** on your bedside table. Fill small, decorative bottles with glittery liquids and label them with romantic runes. It's just colored water, but your partner doesn't need to know that!

5.   Don't forget a sign above the bed that says, **"Fólkvangr: Where love warriors rest."** It's romantic and educational! Add smaller signs with cheesy Viking pick-up lines like "Is that Mjölnir in your pocket, or are you just happy to see me?"

6.   Replace regular **candles** with **rune-carved** ones. Each rune can represent various aspects of love and passion. Just be careful not to accidentally summon anything while setting the mood!

7.   Create a **"Wall of Conquest"** where you and your partner can pin mementos from your romantic "raids" (date nights). Movie tickets, pressed flowers, photos – all are fair game for this romantic plunder display.

THE VIKING PATIO PARADISE

Don't neglect your outdoor space! Turn your balcony or patio into a Norse nature retreat.

1.   Create a mini **"Sacred Grove"** with potted plants. Bonus points if you can find a miniature ash tree to represent Yggdrasil. Name all your plants after Norse gods and talk to them accordingly.

2.   Set up a small **fire pit or brazier**. S'mores taste even better when you pretend they're offerings to the gods. Create a sign designating it as "Muspelheim's Embassy to Midgard."

3.   Hang **wind chimes** made of bones... okay, maybe just bone-shaped pieces of wood or plastic. The creepier the sound, the better. Tell guests it's how you communicate with your Viking ancestors.

4.   Don't forget a **bird feeder** for Odin's ravens, Huginn and Muninn. The real ravens probably won't show up, but the local pigeons will appreciate it. Refer to all visiting birds as "Odin's spies" and act accordingly.

5.   Set up a "**Viking sundial**"—basically, just a stick in a pot of dirt. Tell guests it's how you track time for your raids. They don't need to know you're really checking your phone. Add runes around the base to make it look more authentic.

6.   Create a **"Bifrost Bridge"** leading to your patio. This could be as simple as painting a rainbow path on the ground or as elaborate as stringing rainbow lights overhead.

7.   Install a small water feature and call it your personal **"Well of Urd."** Toss coins in for wishes and pretend you're consulting the Norns every time you look into it.

PART II: VIKING TRANSPORTATION: RAIDING THE ROADS (AND PARKING LOTS)

Now that we've transformed your living space into a budget-friendly Valhalla, it's time to take your Viking lifestyle on the road. After all, what's a Viking without a trusty vessel to carry them to new lands (or at least to the grocery store)?

THE CARSHIP ENTERPRISE
TURNING YOUR CAR INTO A LONGSHIP

Who says you need water to sail? With a little creativity, your car can become the envy of all Vikings, past and present.

1. **Longship Silhouette:** Use removable vinyl decals to create the silhouette of a longship along the sides of your car. Make sure to include the iconic curved prow and stern. **Pro tip:** Make the decals reflective for added safety and Viking bling at night.

2. **Shield Wall:** Attach foam or cardboard "shields" along the sides of your car. Paint them with Norse designs for extra authenticity. Just make sure they're securely fastened – you don't want to leave a trail of shields on the highway.

3. **Dragon Head:** Fashion a removable dragon head for your car's hood. Use lightweight materials like foam or papier-mâché. Remember to remove it before going through a car wash unless you want to give the car wash attendants a real Viking surprise.

4. **Oar Illusion:** Create the illusion of oars sticking out from your car using pool noodles painted brown. Attach them (securely!) to your car's sides. Just be mindful of your new width when parking.

5. **Sail Sunroof:** If you have a sunroof, why not turn it into a sail? Create a removable fabric sail that can be attached when parked. Just remember to take it down before driving unless you want to literally sail down the freeway.

6. **Horn Helmet Hood Ornament:** Replace your boring old hood ornament with a miniature Viking helmet. It's like a hood ornament and a battle cry all in one!

7. **Rune License Plate:** Get a custom license plate with Norse runes. "VKNG RDR" or "FRYA GRL" are sure to turn heads.

8. **Mead Horn cupholders:** Replace your standard cupholders with mead horn holders. How cool! "I'm ready for Valhalla" sipping morning coffee from a horn while stuck in traffic.

THE BICYCLE BERSERKER
VIKING-IFYING YOUR TWO-WHEELER

For the eco-friendly Viking, a bicycle is the perfect blend of personal power and transportation. Here's how to turn your bike into a weapon of mass transportation.

1. **Shield wheel covers:** Create wheel covers that look like Viking shields. Not only do they look cool, but they also protect your spokes from errant tree branches (or enemy arrows).

2. **Handlebar horns:** Attach small horns to your handlebars. They're perfect for alerting pedestrians of your approach or for celebrating particularly epic jumps over curbs.

3. **Fur seat cover:** Replace your standard seat cover with a faux fur one. It's like sitting on a freshly slain beast, but without the mess or ethical concerns.

4. **Saddlebags of holding:** Upgrade your saddlebags to look like leather pouches. Perfect for carrying your

modern Viking essentials like your phone, wallet, and emergency snacks (jerky, obviously).

5. **Raven figurehead:** Attach a small raven figurine to your handlebars. It's like having Odin's own GPS guiding you on your journeys.

6. **Battle cry bell:** Replace your standard bike bell with one that makes a more fearsome sound. A mini gong or a horn would be perfect.

7. **Runic reflectors:** Safety is important, even for Vikings. Replace your standard reflectors with ones shaped like runes. You'll be visible and mystical.

THE SKATEBOARD SAGA
ROLLING WITH THE NORSE

For the Viking on the go, a skateboard can be your trusty steed. Here's how to give it that Norse touch.

1. **Longship deck:** Paint or apply a vinyl wrap to your deck to make it look like a miniature longship. Don't forget the dragon head and tail on the ends!

2. **Runic grip tape:** Cut your grip tape into runic shapes. It's functional and fashionable.

3. **Shield wheels:** Paint your wheels to look like tiny Viking shields. Each rotation is like a mini battle.

4. **Mjölnir truck guards:** Shape your truck guards to look like Thor's hammer. They'll protect your board and possibly grant you the power of thunder (results may vary).

5. **Beard helmet:** Okay, this one's for you, not the board. Get a helmet with an attached fake beard. Safety first, style always.

THE PUBLIC TRANSIT PILLAGER
RAIDING THE BUS AND SUBWAY

Even if you're relegated to public transportation, you can still bring the Viking spirit to your commute.

1. **Collapsible drinking horn:** Bring a collapsible silicone drinking horn for your morning coffee. It's a conversation starter and a fantastic way to freak out your fellow commuters.

2. **Rune-inscribed transit pass:** Decorate your transit pass holder with Norse runes. Maybe it'll magically grant you free rides (Disclaimer: It won't, please pay for your tickets).

3. **Viking-inspired headphones:** Decorate your headphones to look like a miniature Viking helmet. Now you can listen to Viking metal while looking the part.

4. **Fur-lined jacket:** A fur-lined (faux, of course) jacket isn't just warm, it's a terrific way to take up extra space on crowded buses. Personal space is important for a Viking.

5. **Odin's eyepatch:** For those early morning commutes when you can barely keep your eyes open anyway, why not wear an eyepatch? Tell people you sacrificed your eye for wisdom, not that you stayed up too late binge-watching "Vikings."

6.   **Portable feast kit:** Bring a small wooden box filled with Viking-inspired snacks like dried meat, nuts, and fruit. Offer to share with your fellow commuters. You might make some new shield-brothers and shield-sisters.

7.   **Hammer keychain:** Attach a small Thor's hammer to your keychain. It's great for fidgeting during long rides and doubles as a conversation piece.

8.   **Rune stone tablet case:** Decorate your tablet or e-reader case to look like a runestone. Now you're not just reading, you're deciphering ancient Viking wisdom (or, you know, checking your email).

9.   **Viking travel pillow:** Transform a regular travel pillow into a Viking helmet shape. It's perfect for napping on long commutes and makes you look like you're always ready for battle, even when you're drooling in your sleep.

10. **Rune-ify your reading material:** Cover your books or magazines with wrapping paper decorated with Norse designs. Tell curious onlookers you're studying ancient texts.

THE LONGSHIP LAUNCHER
TRANSFORMING YOUR BOAT OR KAYAK

For those lucky enough to have access to actual water, why not turn your watercraft into a genuine Viking vessel?

1.   **Dragon prow:** Attach a removable dragon head to the front of your boat or kayak. Make it detachable for easy storage and to avoid scaring small children at the

beach. Bonus points if you can make it squirt water for extra sea-serpent effect!

2. **Shield railing:** Line the sides of your boat with foam shields. They're decorative and can double as emergency flotation devices. Paint epic battle scenes on each shield to tell the story of your aquatic adventures.

3. **Striped sail:** If you have a sailboat, replace your standard sail with a red and white striped one. It's historically correct and makes you easy to spot on the water. Add a large raven silhouette to the sail to show you're under Odin's protection.

4. **Oar decorations:** Paint your oars or paddles to look like Viking weapons. Each stroke is like a mini battle against the sea. Name your oars after famous Viking warriors for extra motivation during long trips.

5. **Onboard mead horn:** Keep a (waterproof) mead horn on board for mid-journey refreshment. Fill it with water though. Maritime law enforcement tends to frown on actual mead. Use it to perform dramatic toasts to Njord, God of the sea, before each voyage.

6. **Raven flag:** Fly a flag with Odin's ravens from your mast or the back of your kayak. Let Huginn and Muninn guide your journey. Make it double-sided with a kraken design on the reverse for when you're feeling particularly fearsome.

7. **Waterproof rune stickers:** Decorate your hull with waterproof rune stickers. They're decorative and might just grant you Thor's protection on the high seas (or your local lake). Create a "rune of the day" game where you pick a rune before each trip to divine your aquatic fortune.

8. **Viking navigation tools:** Mount a toy compass and spyglass near your steering area. They may not be functional, but they'll make you feel like a true Norse explorer. Practice dramatically pointing to the horizon and shouting "Land ho!" at regular intervals.

9. **Sea chest storage:** Replace any modern storage containers with a rustic wooden chest. It's perfect for holding your modern boating gear while maintaining the Viking aesthetic. BONUS: it doubles as seating for those long voyages to the other side of the lake.

10. **Onboard saga stone:** Bring a large, flat stone and some chalk on your boat trips. Use it to record the "saga" of your journey, complete with exaggerated tales of sea monsters defeated, and new lands discovered (even if it's just that cove you've never noticed before).

PART III: VIKING TRAVEL
RAIDING AND ROAMING ON A BUDGET

Now that we've got your home and transportation sorted, it's time to take your Viking lifestyle on the road. Whether you're planning a weekend getaway or a full-scale invasion (of tourist attractions, of course), here's how to travel like a true Norse warrior without pillaging your savings account.

CHOOSING YOUR RAID DESTINATION

When planning your Viking voyage, consider these budget-friendly options.

1. **Scandinavian-inspired locales:** Can't afford a trip to Norway? Look for towns with Scandinavian heritage closer to home. Many have Viking festivals and Norse-inspired attractions. **Bonus:** You can practice your Old Norse pickup lines on unsuspecting locals.

2. **Natural wonders:** Vikings were connected to nature.
    Find a destination with impressive landscapes like
    fjords, forests, or mountains. Your local state park
    might just become your personal Asgard. Remember
    to loudly proclaim "I name this land... [insert your
    name]'s Vale!" upon arrival. Just don't be surprised if
    park rangers ask you to keep it down.

3. **Historical sites:** Look for destinations with medieval
    history. You might not find actual Viking artifacts, but
    you can pretend that castle was once raided by your
    ancestors. Whisper dramatically to your travel
    companions about the "ghosts of conquests past" at
    every creaky floorboard.

4. **Coastal areas:** Any place with a coast can be a Viking
    destination if you use your imagination. That quiet
    beach town? It's just waiting to be "raided"
    (respectfully and legally, of course). Practice your
    Viking sea-shanties while building epic sandcastle
    fortresses.

5. **Renaissance Faires:** While not strictly Viking, many
    Renaissance Faires have Norse-inspired sections. It's
    like time travel on a budget! Challenge the jousting
    knights to a "friendly" axe-throwing competition.
    (**Note:** Most Renaissance Faires do not actually allow
    axe-throwing. Stick to Turkey legs and mead.)

6. **Iceland-inspired geothermal areas:** If you can't make
    it to the real Iceland, find a local hot spring or
    geothermal area. Soak in the warm waters while
    dramatically reciting the Prose Edda. Just maybe wait
    until you're alone before trying to recreate Snorri
    Sturluson's writing process.

7. **Northern lights viewing spots:** Find a dark sky park
    or northern area where you might catch a glimpse of

the aurora. Pretend you're watching the Valkyries ride across the sky. Bonus points if you can convince other stargazers to join in a spontaneous "Ride of the Valkyries" sing-along.

Packing Like a Norse Nomad

Vikings were known for traveling light (except for all that plunder). Here's how to pack efficiently for your modern-day raid.

1. **The one-bag challenge:** Try to fit everything into a single bag. Pretend you're packing for a longship voyage where space is limited. If it doesn't fit in one reasonably sized duffel bag, you probably don't need it. **Exception:** Your drinking horn. That's a travel essential.

2. **Versatile clothing:** Choose items that can be layered and mixed-and-matched. A simple tunic (t-shirt) can be dressed up with a cloak (jacket) for feasts (dinner out). Pack clothes in neutral colors so you can create different outfits. Think "earthy tones of Midgard" rather than "glittering gold of Asgard."

3. **Compact feast gear:** Bring a collapsible mead horn and a compact wooden bowl and spoon set. You never know when you'll need to feast on the go. Practice dramatically pulling out your feast gear at fast food restaurants. "I shall dine like the Aesir!" you'll declare while pouring your soda into your mead horn.

4. **Travel-sized runestones:** Pack a small set of rune stones for divination on the go. They're like Viking tarot cards, but much easier to pack. Use them to make all your travel decisions. "The runes say we should turn left here... no, your other left."

5. **Portable fur:** A small faux fur throw can serve as a blanket, a pillow, or a fashionable cape for impromptu feasts. Drape it over your shoulders and strut through the hotel lobby like you're entering Odin's great hall.

6. **Viking grooming kit:** Don't forget your beard comb and hair ties for those classic Norse braids. Looking good is half the battle. Include a small mirror for last-minute raid appearance checks.

7. **Inflatable axe:** For when you absolutely must have a weapon but can't get it through airport security. Great for impromptu Viking photoshoots or for threatening unruly luggage that refuses to fit in the overhead compartment.

8. **Norse phrasebook:** Create a small booklet of useful Viking phrases. Include classics like "Where is the nearest mead hall?" and "I swear I'm not actually pillaging; I'm just an enthusiastic tourist."

9. **Travel raven:** Bring a small stuffed raven as your travel companion. Consult it for wisdom and pretend to send messages back home. Huginn, fly swift and true to Ikea, and tell them we need more meatballs!

10. **Pocket sagas:** Print out mini versions of your favorite Norse sagas for travel reading. Dramatically read them aloud at tourist attractions. "And lo, did Thor disguise himself as a bride to retrieve his hammer... much like how I'm disguising myself as a normal tourist to infiltrate this gift shop."

Remember, the key to Viking packing is versatility and a healthy dose of imagination. With these items, you'll be ready for any adventure Midgard throws your way!

BUDGET-FRIENDLY VIKING ACCOMMODATION

Finding affordable lodging fit for a Norse god or goddess.

1. **Hostels:** The modern equivalent of a Viking communal long house. Great for meeting fellow travelers and sharing tales of your adventures. Claim the top bunk by right of conquest (or just by asking politely).

2. **Camping:** Channel your inner Viking explorer by sleeping under the stars. Just try not to pillage your neighboring campsites. Set up your tent like a mini-Viking settlement, complete with a flag bearing your family crest (or hastily drawn raven).

3. **Farm stays:** Many farms offer affordable accommodations. It's like staying in a Viking village, but with indoor plumbing. Offer to help with chores in exchange for your stay, just like a Viking would (except maybe skip the raiding part).

4. **Couchsurfing:** Stay with locals for free. It's like being a Viking guest, minus the obligation to join them in their next raid. Bring a small gift for your hosts, preferably not plundered from their neighbors.

5. **Off-season travel:** Visit popular destinations during the off-season. The weather might be more challenging, but so were Viking voyages. Brave the elements like a true Norse warrior (while secretly appreciating modern heating systems).

6. **Monastery stays:** Some monasteries offer affordable accommodations to travelers. It's historically accurate, as Vikings often visited monasteries (albeit for varied reasons). Promise the monks you're just there to sleep, not to recreate historical events.

7. **University dorms:** Many universities rent out dorm rooms during summer breaks. It's like staying in a training camp for young Viking warriors (or, you know, students).

8. **Hammock camping:** For the truly adventurous Viking, bring a hammock for sleeping outdoors. It's like being cradled in the branches of Yggdrasil itself (but maybe bring bug spray).

Remember, a true Viking can make any accommodation feel like home with the right attitude and enough fur throws!

VIKING-INSPIRED ACTIVITIES ON A BUDGET

You don't need a dragon's hoard of gold to enjoy Viking-style activities.

1. **Hiking:** Explore the local landscape like a Viking scout. Bonus points if you wear a cloak and carry a walking stick. Name every hill you climb after a Norse god. "I claim this mount in the name of Freyja!"

2. **Beach combing:** Search for treasures washed up on the shore. It's like raiding, but legal and environmentally friendly. Create elaborate back stories for each piece of sea glass or driftwood you find.

3. **Local museums:** Many have medieval or cultural sections. Use your imagination to Viking-ify the exhibits. Whisper dramatically to your companions about how you're "casing the joint for a future raid."

4. **Craft workshops:** Look for workshops on traditional crafts like weaving or woodworking. Vikings were skilled artisans, after all. Try to incorporate Norse

designs into everything you make, even if it's just a potholder.

5. **Stargazing:** Learn about Norse constellations and mythology. The night sky was the Viking's GPS. Create your own constellations and epic tales to go with them. "And there's the Loki's Laugh, which always points towards the nearest trickster..."

6. **Local festivals:** Check out local events, especially if they have a historical or cultural focus. You might find a Viking festival if you're lucky! If not, bring the Viking spirit to any festival. Renaissance Faire? Vikings invaded England, close enough!

7. **Nature walks:** Commune with the Norse gods by appreciating nature. That squirrel could be Ratatoskr in disguise. Try to spot as many of Odin's animal associations as you can (ravens, wolves, horses with too many legs...).

8. **Axe throwing:** Many cities now have axe-throwing venues. It's a perfect Viking activity! Just resist the urge to shout, "For Odin!" with every throw. The other patrons might get nervous.

9. **Mead tasting:** Look for local meaderies or bars that serve mead. Conduct a tasting session like you're selecting the perfect brew for Valhalla. Don't forget to dramatically toast the Allfather before each sip.

10. **Viking workout:** Create your own Viking-inspired workout routine using the local environment. Boulders become Thor's weights, trees are for Odin's one-armed pull-ups, and every jog is a chase scene from a Norse saga.

With these activities, you'll have a Viking adventure worthy of the skalds' songs, all without emptying your coin purse!

CHAPTER 8

MODERN VIKING SOCIAL LIFE

Alright, my socially ambitious shield-siblings, it's time to tackle the most perilous challenge of your Viking journey yet: your social life. Now, you might be thinking, "But I'm a fearsome warrior! I don't need a social life!" Well, hate to break it to you, but even Odin himself had to network. How else do you think he got all those ravens to work for him?

In the days of yore, Viking social life was simple. You'd gather in the mead hall, share tales of your latest raids, maybe engage in a friendly axe-throwing competition or two. If you were feeling particularly social, you might raid a neighboring village and make some new "friends." But alas, times have changed. Raid a village these days, and suddenly, you're "breaking the law" and "an international criminal." So unfair.

But fear not, my socially awkward berserker. We're going to navigate the treacherous waters of modern social life with the same courage and creativity our ancestors used to navigate the North Sea. So, grab your mead horn (or your fancy reusable water bottle – hydration is important), and let's dive in!

First up: Dating apps – Swiping right for your shield-maiden (or shield-man, we don't discriminate here in the modern Viking world).

Now, in the old days, Viking courtship was straightforward. You'd impress your potential mate with your raiding skills, your beard-growing abilities, or your talent for composing epic poetry about sea monsters. These days, you've got to compress all that raw Viking energy into a tiny digital profile. Challenge accepted!

Here's how to create the perfect Viking dating app profile.

1. **Profile picture:** Forget shirtless bathroom selfies. You want a picture that screams, "I could totally raid a monastery, but I'm also housetrained." Maybe a nice shot of you axe-throwing... in a business casual outfit.

2. **Bio:** Keep it simple, keep it Viking. "Looking for someone to share mead and epic sagas with. Must love boats and have a high tolerance for sea shanties."

3. **Interests:** Be honest, but strategic. "Interests include long walks on the beach (to scout for potential raid locations), cooking (whole boar over an open fire), and travel (preferably by longship)."

4. **What you're looking for:** "Seeking a shield-maiden/man with a good sword arm and an appreciation for fine furs. Must be willing to help me pillage IKEA for our future home together."

Once you've set up your profile, it's time to start swiping. But beware – the world of Viking online dating is fraught with peril. Here are some red flags to watch out for.

*   If their profile says they're a "Norse god," they're probably not. Even Thor has better things to do than hang out on Tinder.

- Be suspicious of anyone claiming to own a "genuine Viking longship." Unless you live in Scandinavia, they're probably just trying to lure you onto their suspiciously shabby houseboat.

- If they suggest raiding an actual village for your first date, swipe left. Remember, we're modern Vikings. Our raids are strictly metaphorical.

When you do match with someone, remember to keep your conversations Viking-appropriate. Instead of "Netflix and chill," suggest "mead and sagas." Don't ask them out for coffee – invite them to a feast in their honor. And instead of saying "You're hot," try "You look strong enough to bench press a longship." Romance isn't dead; it just speaks Old Norse now.

Now, let's address a crucial point. No matter how much you get into character, it is absolutely NOT okay to kidnap anyone, ever. This includes (but is not limited to) sunbathing women at the beach. I know, I know, some of you are thinking, "But that's how great-great-great-grand pappy Bjorn met great-great-great-grand mammy Astrid!" Well, times have changed, and we've evolved. Today's Vikings understand the importance of consent and respect. So, let's leave the non-consensual "surprise sea voyages" in the past where they belong.

Instead of, you know, literal kidnapping, why not try a cheesy pick-up line? "Excuse me, but I think you dropped something...MY JAW." Okay, maybe not that one. How about, "Are you a Viking raid? Because you've plundered my heart." Still, no? Alright, last try. "Do you believe in love at first sight, or should I walk by in my historically accurate Viking garb again?"

Remember, the goal is to charm your potential shield-maiden or shield-man, not to terrify them. Save the terrifying for your enemies... or for when you have to meet your date's parents.

Moving on to our next topic: How to network at pillage victim support groups. Now, before you get any ideas, let me be clear, we are NOT talking about actual pillaging or actual victims. We're talking about metaphorical pillaging. Think of it as networking at a career fair, but with more fur and mead.

The key to successful networking at these events is to strike the right balance between Viking confidence and modern sensitivity. Here are some tips.

1. **Dress the Part:** You want to look Viking enough to be taken seriously, but not so Viking that people think you're about to start swinging an axe. Think "business casual meets Norse warrior." A nice button-up shirt paired with a tasteful fur vest should do the trick.

2. **Perfect your elevator pitch:** Instead of "Hi, I'm Erik, and I'm in sales," try "Hail! I'm Erik, and I specialize in transferring goods from one owner to another through surprise acquisitions." It's all about the spin.

3. **Bring business cards:** But make them Viking-themed. A nice runestone design always makes an impression. Bonus points if you can actually carve your contact info into a small stone.

4. **Network, don't pillage:** Remember, you're here to make connections, not to raid. So, when someone tells you about their job, don't immediately start planning how to plunder their office. Instead, think about how you can collaborate. "Oh, you're in logistics? I know a thing or two about longship navigation. Perhaps we could discuss this over mead?"

5. **Follow up:** After the event, don't just disappear like a Viking raider into the mist. Send a follow-up message. "It was great meeting you at the pillage... I mean, networking event. I'd love to discuss potential raid... I mean, business opportunities."

Remember, the modern business world is your new raiding ground. Instead of pillaging for gold and silver, you're pillaging for contacts and opportunities. It's all about rebranding!

Now, let's talk about organizing your social gatherings. In the age of Facebook events, how does a modern Viking plan their next raid... Er, I mean, social gathering?

Choose your event name carefully. "Viking Raid on Local Bar" might get you some unwanted attention from local law enforcement. Instead, try something like "Norse-themed Networking Mixer" or "Mead and Mingle: A Viking Social Soirée."

When creating your Facebook event, remember to set the right tone. Here's a template you can use.

"Hear ye, hear ye! (Do Vikings say that? Eh, close enough.)

You are hereby summoned to the grandest gathering this side of Valhalla! Join us for an evening of mead, merriment, and mild pillaging (of the snack table only, please).

WHAT TO EXPECT:
- Feasting fit for a Jarl (potluck style – bring a dish to share).
- Mead tasting (or root beer for our designated longship drivers).
- Friendly competitions of strength and wit (Viking trivia and arm wrestling, anyone?).
- Epic saga sharing (aka showing off your vacation photos).

WHAT TO WEAR: Viking chic is encouraged but not required. Fur, leather, and historically inaccurate horned helmets are all welcome. However, please leave your battle axes at home. We're not barbarians, after all.

REMEMBER: This is a BYOH event (Bring Your Own Horn).

LOCATION: My humble longhouse (aka apartment 3B).

TIME: When the sun is highest in the sky (or 7 PM for those who can't read sundials).

RSVP by carrier raven or by clicking 'attend' below.

May Odin smile upon this gathering!"

When planning your Viking social gathering, remember to be considerate of your non-Viking neighbors. Here are some dos and don'ts.

Do:
- o Inform your neighbors about the gathering (they might want to join).
- o Keep the noise to a reasonable level (save the war cries for the daytime).
- o Clean up any mead spills promptly.

Don't:
- o Try to park a longship in the communal parking lot.
- o Use real swords or axes in your friendly competitions.
- o Sacrifice anything (or anyone) to the Norse gods.

Remember, the goal is to have fun and build your Viking community, not to get evicted or arrested.

Now, let's address the elephant in the room – or should I say, the Gjallarhorn in the great hall. How do you maintain your Viking social life without coming across as, well, a complete lunatic?

The key is to find the right balance between your Viking enthusiasm and social norms. Here are some tips for being a Viking in everyday social situations.

1. **At work:** Instead of shouting "Skål!" every time you finish a task, maybe just do a subtle fist pump. Save the mead-horn-raising for after work hours.

2.   **At the gym:** Channel your inner Viking warrior during your workout but maybe don't challenge everyone to a holmgang (duel). Your local Planet Fitness probably frowns upon axe-throwing.

3.   **At family gatherings:** Regale your relatives with tales of your "raids" (weekend trips) but perhaps don't insist on roasting an entire boar in their backyard.

4.   **On public transportation:** Feel free to stand like a proud Viking warrior, but don't take up more than one seat with your imaginary shield and sword.

5.   **At restaurants:** It's fine to request mead but accept it gracefully if they only have beer. Don't demand to see the manager of Valhalla.

Remember, being a Viking in the modern world is all about attitude. You don't need to wear a horned helmet to the grocery store to prove your Norse credentials. Your Viking spirit should shine through in your confidence, your sense of adventure, and your willingness to try new things (as long as those new things don't involve actual pillaging).

As we wrap up our guide to modern Viking social life, let's take a moment to reflect on what we've learned. We've navigated the treacherous waters of online dating, networked like pros at metaphorical pillage victim support groups, and planned the perfect Viking social gathering. We've learned that being a Viking today is less about swinging axes and more about swinging attitude.

Remember, my socially savvy shield-siblings, the most important thing is to be true to yourself. Whether you're swiping right on dating apps, networking at business events, or just hanging out with friends, let your inner Viking shine. Be bold, be brave, and be ready to regale everyone with tales of your epic deeds (even if those deeds are just successfully assembling IKEA furniture without weeping).

And if anyone gives you strange looks for your Viking enthusiasm? Well, just fix them with your fiercest Norse glare and say, "Odin is cool with it." They'll either be impressed by your dedication or too confused to argue. Either way, you win.

CHAPTER 9

CAREER ADVICE FOR THE MODERN VIKING

Gather 'round, my career-hungry shield-siblings! It's time to tackle the most fearsome beast in the modern world: the job market. Now, I know what you're thinking. "But I'm a Viking! My only skills are pillaging, plundering, and writing epic sagas about pillaging and plundering!" Well, fear not, my horn-helmed friend. As it turns out, those Viking skills of yours are more transferable than you might think.

In this chapter, we're going to explore how to navigate the treacherous waters of the modern job market with the same courage and cunning our ancestors used to navigate the North Sea. So, polish up your resume (or runestone, if you're old school), and let's set sail on your career journey!

First up: Translating your pillaging skills to your LinkedIn profile.

Now, I know LinkedIn can seem as foreign and intimidating as a distant shore ripe for raiding. But think of it as your digital longship, ready to carry you to new career opportunities. The trick is to describe your Viking skills in a way that won't terrify potential employers (or get you arrested). Here's how to Viking-ify your LinkedIn profile.

1) **PROFESSIONAL SUMMARY**

   a) Instead of "Experienced pillager with a track record of successful raids."

   b) Try "Results-driven professional with a proven ability to acquire resources in high-pressure situations."

2) **SKILLS**

   a) Replace "Axe throwing" with "Precision targeting".

   b) "Longship navigation" becomes "Strategic route planning".

   c) "Berserker rage" translates to "Intense focus under pressure".

   d) "Pillaging" is now "Rapid asset acquisition".

   e) "Raid planning" becomes "Project management".

3) **EXPERIENCE**

   a) **Job Title:** Viking Raider Company: Northmen Acquisitions LLC Duration: 793 AD — Present Responsibilities:

      i) Led cross-functional teams in high-stakes acquisition projects.

      ii) Navigated complex international regulations in resource redistribution.

      iii) Developed and implemented strategies for rapid market entry and exit.

      iv) Managed diverse teams in multicultural environments.

v) Excellent record of meeting and exceeding acquisition targets.

4) EDUCATION

a) School of Hard Knocks, Fjord Campus Degree: Master of Pillage Administration (MPA) Relevant Coursework:

i) Advanced Longship Economics.

ii) Conflict Resolution Through Superior Firepower.

iii) Cross-Cultural Negotiations (Saying "Surrender" in 12 Languages).

iv) Ethical Plundering: Balancing Profit and Sustainability.

5) VOLUNTEER EXPERIENCE

a) "Organized annual Raiders Give Back charity pillage with all proceeds going to the 'Mead for Mead-less' foundation."

Remember, the key to a good LinkedIn profile is to highlight your transferable skills. Sure, you may have learned teamwork by rowing a longship, but that doesn't mean you can't apply those skills to leading a project team. Just maybe don't mention the part about motivating your team with threats of walking the plank.

Now, let's talk about startup ideas. Because let's face it, in today's world, if you can't find a job that fits your Viking skills, why not create one?

You mentioned "Uber, but for longships," and I've got to say, you might be onto something there. Let's flesh out this idea and a few others.

1) **"RAID SHARE"** (Uber for longships)

   a) **Tagline:** "Why sail alone when you can raid together?"

   b) **How it works:** Users can request a ride on a local longship for their daily commute or weekend raids. Drivers (or should we say, captains) with their own longships can sign up to provide rides. Here are some specific ideas.

      i) **"Plunder Pool":** Carpooling, but for raiders.

      ii) **"Raid Roulette":** For the adventurous types who don't care where they're raiding, just that they're raiding.

      iii) **"Mead-o-Meter":** Rate your captain's horn of mead (remember, don't drink and sail!).

2) **"AIRBNB & PILLAGE"**

   a) **Tagline:** "Stay, plunder, leave a 5-star review!"

   b) **How it works:** This revolutionary app combines short-term vacation rentals with old-school Viking raiding. Users can book a stay in a foreign land, with the added bonus of being able to pillage the neighborhood (ethically and sustainably, of course). Features include:

      i) **"Loot Lockers"** for secure storage of your plunder.

      ii) **"Raid Ratings"** to help you choose the best pillaging spots.

      iii) **"Alibi Assistance"** for when the local authorities start asking questions.

2) **"VIKING DASH"**

   a) **Tagline:** "From fjord to table in 30 minutes or less!" Why settle for boring old food delivery when you can have your mead and mutton delivered by a longship?

   b) **How it works:** This app connects hungry modern Vikings with local mead halls and Viking-themed restaurants. Features include:

      i) **"Raid My Fridge"** option for when you're too tired to pillage your own kitchen.

      ii) **"Feast Mode"** for large order discounts.

      iii) **"Shield Wall Delivery"** guaranteeing your food arrives hot and un-pillaged.

2) **"LINKEDIN, BUT FOR VIKINGS"**

   a) **Tagline:** "Networking? No, Norseworking!" A professional networking site specifically for the Viking community.

   b) **How it works:** Users can connect with fellow raiders, share tips on the best pillaging spots, and even find their next shield-maiden or shield-man. Features include:

      i) **"Skill endorsements"** for things like "axe sharpening" and "ship building".

      ii) **"Raid recommendations"** from satisfied pillaging partners.

      iii) **"Valhalla headhunters"** for executive-level Viking job placements.

   The key to a successful startup is identifying a need in the market and filling it. And if that need happens to be longshipbased transportation or ethical pillaging services, well, who are we to argue with the free market?

Now, let's navigate the treacherous waters of office politics, Viking style. In the old days, if you had a disagreement with a coworker, you could challenge them to a holmgang (duel) and be done with it. Unfortunately, HR frowns upon that sort of thing these days. So how does a Viking handle office politics without resorting to actual battle axes?

1) **The art of the subtle threat:** Instead of saying "Meet my demands or face my axe," try "I'm sure we can come to an agreement that benefits us both." The implied threat of Viking retribution is there, but it's subtle enough to maintain plausible deniability.

2) **Form your own shield wall:** In Viking battles, warriors would form a shield wall for protection. In the office, form alliances with your coworkers. There's strength in numbers, whether you're facing down Saxon hordes or passive-aggressive emails.

3) **The carved rune stone approach:** Vikings used rune stones to commemorate notable events. In the office, document everything. Every agreement, every decision, every time Karen from accounting steals your lunch from the break room fridge. It's like leaving a runestone, but with less heavy lifting.

4) **Raid and retreat:** Sometimes, Vikings would perform quick, surgical strikes and then disappear before the enemy could retaliate. In office politics, learn when to make your point and when to strategically retreat. Win the battle but avoid the war.

5) **The mead hall meeting:** Vikings would often solve disputes over a horn of mead. While we don't recommend bringing alcohol into the workplace, the principle of solving issues in a more relaxed, neutral setting still

applies. Suggest a coffee meeting instead of a confrontation by the water cooler.

6) **Channel your inner Loki:** No, we're not suggesting you unleash chaos in the office. But a little clever wordplay and strategic mischief can go a long way in office politics. Just be careful not to take it too far, or you might find yourself metaphorically chained to a rock with a snake dripping venom on you (or in a long meeting with HR, which is basically the same thing).

Remember, the goal in office politics is not to crush your enemies and hear the lamentations of their women (or men, we're equal opportunity Vikings here). It's to create a work environment where you can thrive and advance your career. Think less "blood eagle" and more "strategic alliance building."

Now, let's address a crucial aspect of the modern Viking's career: Translating your sword skills to the art of sandwich making. That's right, we're talking about becoming a Subway Sandwich Artist.

You might think that your skills with a sword have no place in the world of foot-long subs and cookie upsells, but you couldn't be more wrong. Here's how your Viking sword skills translate to sandwich artistry.

1) **Precision cutting:** Your ability to wield a sword with pinpoint accuracy translates perfectly to slicing tomatoes and onions with samurai-like precision. Your sandwiches will be the envy of the entire franchise.

2) **Speed and efficiency:** The quick, decisive movements needed in sword combat are the same ones that will help you assemble sandwiches at lightning speed during the lunch rush. You'll be the "Flash of the Flatbread".

3) **Handling pressure:** If you can keep your cool while facing down a horde of angry Saxons, you can certainly handle a line of hangry office workers on their lunch break.

4) **Creative combinations:** Just as you had to creatively combine your sword techniques to defeat various foes, you'll need to creatively combine ingredients to satisfy diverse customer tastes. Think of each sandwich as a new battle strategy.

5) **Maintaining your weapon:** The care you took in maintaining your sword translates to keeping your work area clean and your ingredients fresh. A clean sandwich line is a happy sandwich line.

6) **Intimidation tactics:** While we don't recommend actually intimidating customers, the confident stance and fierce gaze you developed as a Viking warrior will serve you well when dealing with indecisive customers. "You want the Italian B.M.T., trust me."

WHEN LISTING THIS EXPERIENCE ON YOUR RESUME, TRY SOMETHING LIKE THIS.

Job Title: Sandwich Blade Master (aka Subway Sandwich Artist) Duration: 2023 — Present

Responsibilities:

- Wielded blade-like instruments to craft edible masterpieces for discerning clientele

- Strategically deployed flavor combinations to conquer customer cravings

- Defended the honor of the Six-Inch Sub against the villainous forces of hunger

- Always supported a clean and orderly battlefield (sandwich preparation area)

- Successfully upsold cookies and drinks using techniques perfected in high-stakes negotiations

Remember, whether you're swinging a sword or spreading mayo, it's all about confidence, skill, and not accidentally cutting off your own fingers.

Now, let's explore another career path perfect for the modern Viking: Security Guard.

Think about it – who better to guard valuable assets than someone whose ancestors made a living acquiring (or, ahem, "redistributing") valuable assets? Here's how to Viking-up your security guard career:

1) **Intimidating presence:** Your Viking stature and fierce glare will make potential troublemakers think twice. Who needs a uniform when you've got a beard that could house a family of sparrows?

2) **Perimeter checks:** Think of it as patrolling the borders of your territory, just like Vikings guarded their settlements. Except instead of watching for rival clans, you're watching for shoplifters and rowdy teenagers.

3) **Surveillance skills:** Those long hours spent as a Viking lookout, scanning the horizon for potential raid targets, translates perfectly to monitoring security cameras. Except the view is probably less scenic.

4) **Conflict resolution:** Your ancestors might have resolved conflicts with axes, but you can use those same intimidation skills to de-escalate situations with nothing more than a stern look and a firmly worded warning.

5) **Asset protection:** Instead of raiding monasteries for their gold, you're protecting the modern equivalent—the electronics section at Best Buy.

6) **Communication skills:** The ability to shout orders over the din of battle serves you well when trying to be heard over the cacophony of a rowdy crowd at a concert or sporting event.

WHEN DESCRIBING THIS JOB ON YOUR RESUME, TRY SOMETHING LIKE:

Job Title: Asset Protection Specialist (Viking Security Division) Duration: 2024-Present

Responsibilities:

- Maintained vigilant watch over assigned territory, deterring potential invaders with imposing presence

- Utilized advanced Norse surveillance techniques to monitor for suspicious activity

- Employed Viking-inspired conflict resolution strategies to maintain peace and order

- Protected valuable assets with the ferocity of a dragon guarding its hoard

- Coordinated with fellow warriors (team members) to ensure comprehensive site security

Remember, as a Viking security guard, your job is to prevent pillaging, not engage in it. It's a bit of a career shift, but hey, even Odin had to adapt with the times.

As we wrap up our journey through the modern Viking career landscape, let's take a moment to reflect on what we've learned. We've discovered that those Viking skills of yours – the courage, the cunning, the ability to rock an impressive beard – are more valuable in today's job market than you might have thought.

Whether you're crafting the perfect LinkedIn profile, launching the next big Viking-inspired startup, navigating office politics with the finesse of a master tactician, assembling sandwiches with the precision of a master swordsman, or guarding assets with the ferocity of a berserker, you've got what it takes to conquer the modern job market.

Remember, my career-hungry shield-siblings, the most important thing is to approach your job search with the same spirit of adventure and fearlessness that led our ancestors to sail into unknown waters. Be bold in your career choices. Be innovative in how you apply your Viking skills to modern problems. And always, always be ready to regale your coworkers with tales of your epic deeds (even if those deeds are just successfully fixing the office printer without having a meltdown).

And if anyone ever questions your Viking-inspired approach to your career? Well, just fix them with your fiercest Norse glare and say, "Odin approves of my career choices." They'll either be impressed by your dedication or too confused to argue. Either way, you win.

Now, if you'll excuse me, I have a LinkedIn profile to update. I think "Pillaging Consultant" has a nice ring to it, don't you? Skål, and happy job hunting!

CHAPTER 10

CONCLUSION: LIVING YOUR BEST NORSE LIFE

Well, my fjord-faring friends, we've come to the end of our saga. We've pillaged our way through fashion, feasted on knowledge about Norse cuisine, and raided the job market with our Viking skills. But the question remains of how do we take all this newfound Viking wisdom and apply it to our daily lives without, you know, getting arrested or socially ostracized?

Fear not, for this last chapter will guide you through the treacherous waters of modern Viking living. We'll explore how to embrace your inner Norse warrior while keeping both feet firmly planted in the 21st century (unless, of course, you're doing a particularly enthusiastic Viking squat). So, grab your horn of mead (or artisanal craft beer, we don't judge), and let's dive into living your best Norse life!

First up: Embracing your inner Viking while avoiding cultural appropriation charges.

You might be thinking, "But I bought this horned helmet and fake beard on eBay! I've watched every episode of 'Vikings' twice! I'm practically Norse royalty!" Slow down there, Leif

Erikson. While your enthusiasm is admirable, we need to approach this with the cunning of Odin himself.

The key to embracing your inner Viking without offending anyone is to focus on the values and spirit of Viking culture, rather than just the surface-level aesthetics. Here's how.

1) **Embrace the Viking work ethic:** Vikings were known for their craftsmanship and work ethic. Channel this by putting your all into everything you do, whether it's your job, your hobbies, or your attempt to build a longship in your backyard.

2) **Adopt the spirit of exploration:** Vikings were great explorers. Satisfy your wanderlust by trying new things, visiting unexplored places, or even just taking a different route to work. Who knows? You might discover America. (Spoiler alert: someone beat you to it.)

3) **Value community and loyalty:** Vikings had a keen sense of community. Foster close relationships with your friends and family. Host regular feasts (potlucks work too) and always have your friends' backs in times of need.

4) **Appreciate nature:** Vikings had a deep connection with nature. Take time to enjoy the outdoors, whether it's hiking, camping, or just cloud-watching in your local park. Just maybe skip the human sacrifices to ensure a good harvest.

5) **Learn about actual Norse history and mythology:** Instead of just wearing Thor's hammer because it looks cool, learn about its significance. Read the Eddas, study Norse mythology, and appreciate the complexity of Viking culture.

Remember, cultural appreciation involves respect, understanding, and engagement with the actual culture. It's not about playing dress-up or using "Viking" as an excuse to act rowdy at your local bar. Unless that bar is an actual Viking mead hall, in which case, rowdiness may be appropriate. (NOTE: Your local TGI Friday's does not count as a mead hall, no matter how many antiques they have on the walls.)

FINDING YOUR CLAN IN THE URBAN JUNGLE

In the days of old, Vikings had their clans and villages. In today's world, it can feel like you're a lone warrior adrift in a sea of indifference (also known as city life). But fear not! Your clan is out there. You just need to know where to look.

1) **Join a Viking reenactment group:** Yes, they exist, and they're probably a lot more historically accurate than your eBay horned helmet. It's a wonderful way to meet fellow Norse enthusiasts and learn authentic Viking skills.

2) **Attend Renaissance Faires:** While not strictly Viking, many Ren faires have Norse-themed areas or events. Plus, it's one of the few places where carrying around a turkey leg and speaking in a vaguely European accent is socially acceptable.

3) **Find a local Norse pagan group:** If you're interested in the spiritual aspects of Viking culture, these groups can provide community and deeper understanding. Just remember it's about spirituality, not an excuse to drink mead and shout "Skål!" (Although that might happen too.)

4) **Join a Viking-inspired fitness class:** From "Viking Yoga" to "Berserker Bootcamps," Viking-themed workouts are becoming popular. It's a wonderful way to meet people and get fit enough to actually wear that chain mail you bought.

5) **Start a Norse book club:** Gather some friends and read Norse sagas together. It's like a regular book club, but with more epic battles and fewer tear-jerking romances. (Unless you count Odin's pursuit of wisdom as a tear-jerking romance. Fair enough.).

6) **Volunteer for coastal clean-ups:** Channel the Viking connection to the sea by helping keep your local beaches and waterways clean. It's like raiding, but instead of taking things, you're taking away trash.

Remember, your clan doesn't have to be exclusively Viking-obsessed (although it's cool if they are). The important thing is to find people who appreciate your interests and support your journey. After all, even Odin needed his ravens.

Now, let's address a critical point: It's not about the gold you plunder, but the friends you make along the way.

Sure, Vikings had a reputation for raiding and acquiring wealth, but the real treasure was the strong bonds they formed with their fellow warriors. In your modern Viking life, focus on building relationships and creating experiences, not just accumulating stuff.

1) **Host regular feasts:** Invite friends over for potluck dinners. Bonus points if you serve mead and eat traditional Norse dishes. (Maybe warn your guests before serving fermented shark, though.)

2) **Plan adventures:** Organize hiking trips, camping weekends, or even just urban exploration days with your friends. It's not quite the same as sailing to unknown lands, but it'll scratch that Viking exploration itch.

3) **Collaborate on projects:** Whether it's building furniture, creating art, or planning events, working together on something strengthens bonds. It's like building a longship, but with less risk of splinters.

4) **Share skills:** Instruct your friends on something you're good at and let them teach you in return. It's like the Viking tradition of passing down crafts, but instead of learning to forge swords, you might learn to code or make artisanal bread.

5) **Be there in times of need:** Vikings valued loyalty above all. Be the friend who helps move furniture, who listens during tough times, who brings soup when someone's sick. It's less glamorous than battling frost giants, but just as heroic.

Remember, at the end of the day, it's these connections and experiences that will make your life rich, not the number of Instagram followers you have or how authentic your Viking costume is.

Now, let's delve into a crucial aspect of living your best Norse life: eschewing modern utensils and embracing the Viking way of dining. That's right, we're talking about eating with your hands, my messy-fingered friends!

In Viking times, forks were about as common as smartphones and indoor plumbing (which is to say, not at all). Our Norse ancestors ate with their hands, knives, and occasionally spoons. So, if you genuinely want to embrace the Viking lifestyle, it's time to get hands-on with your food. Here's how to do it without completely alienating your friends and family.

1) **Choose your battles:** While eating a salad with your hands might be a bit much, foods like bread, meat, and certain vegetables are perfect for hand-to-mouth action. Start with finger foods and work your way up to full meals.

2) **Master the art of the knife:** Vikings used knives not just for cutting, but also as a utensil. Learn to spear your food with your knife for that authentic Norse dining

experience. (**Note**: Maybe don't try this at fancy restaurants or your grandmother's house).

3) **Embrace the mess**: Eating with your hands is going to get messy. That's part of the fun! Just keep some wet wipes nearby for when things get too Viking-y.

4) **The two-handed technique**: Use your dominant hand for eating and keep your other hand clean for pouring drinks or gesticulating wildly as you regale your dining companions with tales of your mighty deeds.

5) **Know your limits**: While Vikings might have eaten everything with their hands, there are some modern foods that just don't lend themselves to this approach. No one wants to see you trying to eat soup with your bare hands. Know when to surrender to the spoon.

6) **The washing ritual**: Vikings were actually quite concerned with cleanliness, especially when it came to eating. Keep a bowl of water and a towel nearby to wash your hands before and after the meal. It's not just hygienic; it's historically accurate!

Now, I know what you're thinking. "But what about my job? I can't show up to business lunches eating like a Viking raider!" Fear not, my professionally minded berserker. Here are some tips for maintaining your Viking eating habits in the modern world.

1) **The office lunch**: Opt for sandwiches, wraps, or other easily hand-held foods. Your coworkers will just think you're really committed to the "grab and go" lunch lifestyle.

2) **Date night**: Maybe save the full Viking dining experience for after you've secured a second date. Nothing shows

"I'm not ready for a relationship" quite like gnawing on a turkey leg with your bare hands on a first date.

3) **Family dinner:** Start slow. Maybe begin with a "Viking night" where everyone eats with their hands. Who knows? It might become a fun family tradition. (Or a story your kids tell their therapist later. It could go either way).

4) **Fine dining:** Okay, this one's tough. Maybe just stick to the provided utensils when you're at a Michelin-starred restaurant. Even Odin knew when to blend in.

Remember, the key to living your best Norse life is balance. You don't have to eat every meal like you're at a Viking feast. But incorporating this practice into your life when appropriate can be a fun way to connect with your inner Viking. Plus, it's a friendly conversation starter.

"Oh, this? Just embracing my Norse heritage. Pass the wet wipes, would you?"

Now, let's address the elephant in the room – or should I say, the Gjallarhorn in the great hall. How do you maintain your Viking lifestyle without becoming a walking, talking anachronism?

The key is to find modern equivalents for Viking practices and values. Here are some ideas.

1) Instead of raiding monasteries, raid your local **library** for knowledge. It's less lucrative, but also less likely to result in excommunication.

2) Rather than sailing the seas in a longship, try **kayaking or paddleboarding.** It's like Viking exploration, but with more life jackets and less scurvy.

3) Instead of writing runes, **try learning** coding. It's the modern equivalent of a mystical, powerful language that few understand.

4) Rather than becoming a berserker on the battlefield, channel that energy into your workout routine. **Cross-fit** is basically modern berserking, right?

5) Instead of raiding for gold and silver, **invest in cryptocurrency.** It's just as volatile as Viking-era economies, but with fewer swords involved.

Remember, being a modern Viking isn't about recreating the past; it's about taking the best parts of Viking culture and applying them to your life today. It's about facing challenges with courage, valuing community, and loyalty, and always being ready for adventure (even if that adventure is just trying a new coffee shop).

As we come to the end of our saga, let's recap the key points of living your best Norse life.

1) Embrace Viking values, not just Viking aesthetics.

2) Find your modern clan and build strong relationships.

3) Focus on experiences and connections, not just accumulating stuff.

4) Don't be afraid to get a little messy (especially when eating).

5) Balance your Viking practices with modern life.

6) Always be ready for adventure, whether big or small.

7) Learn about actual Norse history and culture.

8) Approach challenges with courage and creativity.

9) Value loyalty, community, and personal growth.

10) Most importantly, have fun with it!

Remember, my fellow Vikings-at-heart, living your best Norse life isn't about perfectly recreating the past. It's about taking the spirit of Viking culture – the bravery, the curiosity, the passionate sense of community – and applying it to your modern life. It's about facing your daily challenges with the courage of a warrior facing down a frost giant. It's about approaching new experiences with the excitement of a Viking seeing a new shore. And yes, it's about occasionally eating with your hands and growing an impressive beard (if you're able).

And finally, my dear Viking enthusiasts, there's one last, crucial step in fully embracing your Norse lifestyle. You must switch your allegiance to the Minnesota Vikings as your favorite football team. That's right, it's time to trade in whatever inferior, non-Norse-named team you've been rooting for and join the purple and gold hoarde.

Now, I know what you're thinking. "But I've been a fan my team my whole life!" Well, guess what? Vikings were all about conquering new territories and adapting to new situations. Consider this your personal raid on the NFL. It's time to don your purple jersey (it goes great with your beard), paint your face, and practice your best "SKOL" chant.

Sure, being a Vikings fan might come with its share of heartbreak and missed field goals but look on the bright side – it's excellent practice for the fatalism inherent in Norse mythology. Just think of each season as Ragnarök, and you'll be emotionally prepared for anything. Plus, where else can you watch modern-day warriors battle it out in a stadium that looks like it could have been designed by Norse gods themselves?

So, raise your horn (or your foam finger) and pledge your loyalty to the Minnesota Vikings. It's not just a team choice; it's the last step in your Viking transformation. And hey, if they ever make it to the Super Bowl, you can claim it as a successful raid on Valhalla itself. SKOL!

Your Viking journey doesn't end with the closing of this book. In fact, it's just beginning. Every day is an opportunity to raid the world for new experiences, to forge strong bonds with your clan, and to write your own saga.

So go forth, my modern Vikings. Raid your local farmers market with the same enthusiasm your ancestors raided coastal villages. Navigate office politics with the strategic mind of a Viking chieftain. Approach your fitness goals like you're training for Ragnarök.

And if anyone gives you strange looks for your Viking enthusiasm? Well, just fix them with your fiercest Norse glare and say, "Skål!" Because at the end of the day, living your best Norse life is about being true to yourself, embracing adventure, and not taking life too seriously.

Now, if you'll excuse me, I have a fjord to explore. Okay, it's actually just a really big puddle in my backyard, but with the right mindset, anything can be a Viking adventure.

May Odin smile upon your journey, may Thor grant you strength, and may Loki give you just enough mischief to keep things interesting. Skål, and happy Viking-ing!

ABOUT THE AUTHOR

KEVIN B. DIBACCO

Kevin's life story is a powerful testament to the resilience of the human spirit. As a writer, Kevin draws from his experiences to share invaluable lessons on overcoming adversity and the temptation to quit. His words carry the weight of someone who has faced unimaginable challenges and emerged stronger, wiser, and more compassionate.

From a young age, Kevin's health struggles began, and he found himself facing one medical battle after another. By his 30s, he had endured a staggering 10 major medical procedures, including multiple knee operations, back surgeries, hip replacements, and treatment for an aggressive brain tumor. Even as he was writing his book, Kevin was struck by COVID-19, which led to pneumonia and daily nebulizer treatments. Lesser men might have given up, but Kevin refused to see himself as a victim of circumstance.

Through each diagnosis and rehabilitation, Kevin made a conscious choice to reframe adversity as an opportunity for growth. He focused on the small wins, visualizing himself healed and happy, and leaning on his deep faith and the support of loved ones during the darkest times. When fear or hopelessness crept in, he turned to prayer, uplifting books, and encouraging sayings to find the strength to take the next step forward.

As he navigated his journey, Kevin discovered the transformative power of the mind and positive thinking. He realized that by controlling his inner world—his thoughts, beliefs, and visualizations—he could shape his outer reality. This profound insight became the foundation for his book, in which he shares his medical battles alongside the techniques he used to stay grounded in positivity.

Kevin's book is not a theoretical exploration of resilience; it is a deeply personal account of his struggles and triumphs. He provides practical exercises to help readers overcome negative self-talk, face their fears, and visualize their desired outcomes. His message is one of hope and empowerment: regardless of what life throws at us, we have the power to choose our response.

Through his writing, Kevin aims to inspire others facing their battles to tap into their inner reserves of strength. He believes that by reframing difficulties as opportunities for growth and committing to personal development, we can overcome any obstacle, including those within our minds.

Kevin's story is a shining example of the human capacity for resilience and the power of the human spirit. His words serve as a reminder that, no matter how many times we are knocked down, we always have the choice to get back up. In sharing his journey, Kevin hopes to inspire others to keep going, even in the face of insurmountable odds.

Introduction: Food as Your Secret Weapon for Health and Performance

Hey there! Welcome to "Eat To Heal: A Practical Guide to Nourishing Your Body and Treating Disease Through Food.

" I'm thrilled you've picked up this book, and I can't wait to share with you the incredible power of food to transform your health, boost your performance, and even change your life.

Now, you might be wondering, "Who's this person, and why should I listen to him about food and health?" Well, allow me to introduce myself. I've been an athlete since I could walk. From Little League to high school sports, I've always been drawn to the thrill of competition and the satisfaction of pushing my body to its limits. But it wasn't until I discovered powerlifting and bodybuilding that I really found my groove.

Picture this: a chubby kid who could barely bench press the bar, transforming into a competitive powerlifter who could deadlift more than twice his body weight. Yeah, that was me. And let me tell you, that journey taught me a thing or two about the importance of what you put into your body.

I remember my first powerlifting meet like it was yesterday. I was nervous as hell, my palms sweating as I approached the platform. But as soon as I wrapped my hands around that bar, something clicked. The months of training, the careful attention to nutrition—it all came together in that moment. When I successfully lifted that weight, setting a personal record, I knew I was hooked.

As a competitive powerlifter, I quickly learned that food wasn't just fuel—it was the foundation of my performance. The right nutrition could mean the difference between setting a new personal record and falling short. And as I transitioned into bodybuilding and eventually became a trainer, I saw firsthand how dramatically the right (or wrong) food choices could impact not just performance but health and well-being.

But here's the kicker: despite being immersed in the world of fitness and nutrition, I still had a lot to learn about food as medicine. Sure, I knew all about protein shakes and carb-loading, but the idea that food could heal the body? That was a game-changer for me.

My "aha" moment came when I was dealing with some nagging injuries and inflammation that just wouldn't quit, no matter how much I stretched or how many ice baths I took. A nutritionist friend suggested I investigate anti-inflammatory foods, and, skeptical but desperate, I gave it a shot. Lo and behold, within a few weeks of tweaking my diet, I noticed a significant improvement. My recovery time shortened, my energy levels shot up, and I even started sleeping better.

That experience opened my eyes to the healing power of food, and I've been on a mission ever since to learn everything I can about using nutrition to optimize health and performance. And let me tell you, it's been one heck of a ride.

Kevin is a member of Best Selling Authors International and Independent Author Network.

You can visit his association pages at:

https://bestsellingauthorsinternational.org/authors/kevin-b-dibacco/

https://www.independentauthornetwork.com/kevin-b-dibacco.html

Follow Kevin's latest releases at these websites!

https://kbd.allauthor.com

www.ptbooksinc.com

BOOKS BY KEVIN DIBACCO

100 Unhealthy Foods

Back Care Made Easy: Simple Stretches and Exercises for Everyone

Bad Air: What Are We Breathing?

Badge of Horror

Being Weird: Unleash Your Inner Weirdo and Conquer the World

Chemicals in Our Food: What's Really on Your Plate?

Coffee: The Magic Brew

Dare to Believe: Building Unshakeable Confidence in All You Do

Desk Duty Fitness

Fitness Decoded: Unlocking the Secrets to Healthiness and Happiness at Any Age!

From Doubt to Believing: Removing the Doubt Obstacle in Our Life

Grip Strength: An Indicator of Your Overall Health

History and Evolution of Weightlifting and Equipment

Hold the Power

Hug It Out: Healing Through Hugging

Hysometrics

Hysterical Strength: The Extraordinary Display of Super Human Strength

I Can, I Will, I Must!

Indie Filmmaking In the Real World

The Confident Warrior: How to Cultivate Confidence in Everyday Life, Then Use It!

The Gabardine Gang: Power and Betrayal in Hartford's Mob

The Great Dimming: The Modern IQ Decline

The Handshake Around the World

The Lost Art of Logical Thinking

The Mozart Mind Effect

The Real World Guide to Digital Filmmaking

They Said What? Some of the Worst Predictions Ever Made!

The Symphony of the Soul: Classical Music and the Impact on Our Mood

Understanding and Overcoming Depression

Unsafe at Any Dose

Unstoppable: Success Through Persistence

We All Need Hope: Where There's Hope, There's a Way Forward

What is the Happiest Country on Earth?

Your Body Recipe: A Captivating Look at What Makes Us Human

FILMS BY KEVIN DIBACCO

Dark Minds (Sci-Fi Thriller)

Early Grave (Horror; Suspense)

www.ingramcontent.com/pod-product-compliance
Lightning Source LLC
Chambersburg PA
CBHW020411150626
46554CB00013B/636